one good life

one good life

MY TIPS, MY WISDOM, MY STORY

Jill Nystul

G. P. Putnam's Sons

New York

PUTNAM

G. P. PUTNAM'S SONS
Publishers Since 1838
Published by the Penguin Group
Penguin Group (USA) LLC
375 Hudson Street
New York, New York 10014

USA · Canada · UK · Ireland · Australia
New Zealand · India · South Africa · China

penguin.com
A Penguin Random House Company

ISBN 978-0-399-16781-2

Printed in the United States of America
1   3   5   7   9   10   8   6   4   2

Book design by Meighan Cavanaugh

To my husband, Dave Nystul,

our children, Erik, Britta, Kell, and Sten,

and my parents, Carole and Richard Warner.

With love.

When everything seems like an uphill struggle, just picture the view from the top.

—*Unknown*

contents

---

prologue

My forty-sixth birthday seems like yesterday, and yet it also seems like a lifetime ago. The date was February 20, 2008. It was not merely a birthday. In fact, it was a rebirth. As birthdays go, forty-six is not one of those overwhelming milestones that make us cringe and dread the turning of a decade. But for me, that birthday was a most auspicious event: It was the day that I graduated from the Ark of Little Cottonwood, a residential treatment facility in Utah. It was close to home and also very far away. I had entered the Ark seventy-eight days before, on December 5.

How I came to the Ark is a long story. The short version is that about ten years before, when I was in my mid-thirties and married to a great guy, Dave, with whom I have four wonderful kids—Erik, Britta, Kell, and Sten—and seemingly had everything that anyone could have wanted, I was miserable. Amorphously, absolutely, and horribly miserable for no reason that I could really explain. All I knew was that I wanted more and needed more and that more was something indefinable and elusive. I felt like I needed to escape something but I didn't know what. The utter confusion and feeling of being completely lost and not knowing why or how to fix it was too much to bear. So I turned to that ubiquitous social lubricant: alcohol.

I could give you a litany of reasons and excuses for why I drank. It's true that I had a great deal of anxiety after each of my children was born. It wasn't postpartum depression. It was postpartum anxiety, where I had a constant sense of impending doom and bouts of nearly paralyzing panic attacks. My doctor prescribed Prozac, and although it eased the panic attacks, it suppressed my libido, and that was like pouring fuel on a fire. The truth is, my marriage was on the rocks before I started drinking. Yes, the pun there is intentional, since levity often makes what was once painful for me seem less so as I look back. Ultimately, after twenty years of marriage, my husband and I separated for a year. With work, we reconciled and healed. Still, I remained anxious. I turned to food as a coping mechanism and suddenly I was dealing with weight gain. Ironically, I didn't gain weight during my pregnancies, but after each one, I added on more postpartum weight. I was sleep-deprived. And I was conflicted: I loved being at home with my babies, and although I also wanted to go back to work, the thought of going back to work made me anxious. My second son, Kell, was diagnosed with diabetes at the age of two and a half. I have battled foot pain since I was sixteen, when I was diagnosed with a nonmalignant tumor on the bottom of my foot. It was successfully treated with radiation therapy, but wouldn't you just know it, while everything else was happening and my life seemed as though it was spinning out of control, that wound site on the bottom of my foot reopened and refused to heal despite two skin grafts. Thirty dives in a hyperbaric chamber finally healed my foot. By this time, my "turning to alcohol" morphed into full-fledged abuse.

Despite all this, I make no excuses. I suppose that from the very first time I stood up in an Alcoholics Anonymous meeting and stated, "My name is Jill and I am an alcoholic," I began the process of taking responsibility for myself and my actions. It was Step Four of the twelve-step program that instructed me to fearlessly take a moral inventory of myself. I remember the very first time that I took that palliative drink. So many things were building up inside and the demons were daring me as I drank with the sole and deliberate intention of numbing the pain. The remedy worked that day for the simple reason that when our senses are altered, we feel less pain. Sometimes we feel no pain at all. I was anesthetized. Let's face it: When you're passed out, you feel nothing. And so the sorrow would leave until I sobered up, and then the next time it crept up, I would reach for the bottle again. I became caught in the vicious cycle.

"Hiding in a bottle" and "drowning sorrows" are clichés because they are facts: Alcohol as a painkiller provides false and temporary sedation. So on and on I went, seeking solace in the bottle, until my family gathered together and staged an intervention. My husband and children found the help that I needed and couldn't find for myself. I didn't make it easy for them. It was like trying to corral a wild mare. But somewhere in my alcohol-addicted brain, I knew they were right and there was no other choice but to get help in a place that was safe and dry and could make me whole again.

I often think that if not for my family, I would either be dead or in jail. If not for my amazing family and the belief that I now hold so dear in a Higher Power, I have been given a second chance. Call the Higher Power what you will: I just feel there is something or someone out there or up there, along with my family and the angels who worked as counselors at the Ark, who helped me to save myself.

I share my story not because I am unique and crave the spotlight, but quite the opposite. I share because I know that there are many like me who are scything the same path I was. I want those people to know that they are not alone—whether they are addicts or love an addict. Addiction of any kind is not shameful. It is neither deliberate nor meant to harm. It is also conquerable. I never say that I "was" an addict. I emphatically state that my addiction remains in a current state. I must be vigilant. I must be aware that I could easily slip. My battle is one that I fight every day, and I do so one day at a time. At the end of each day, I take great joy as I emerge triumphant.

During my stay at the Ark, the counselors taught me many important things, not the least of which was the need to find my passion and pursue it. The notion of uncovering my passion was not just a suggestion; it was mandatory if I wanted to stay sober. As a former broadcast journalist, I knew that communication was my passion and—here's where the irony comes in—I was able to communicate with everyone except myself. That's when the bottle became the wrong kind of friend. With the help of the counselors at the Ark, my passion became a daily journal that morphed into a blog that became a public website. There were days when my passion was driven and other days when I thought my excitement as I recovered was all just smoke and mirrors. But I stuck with the intention, focused on the passion, and gave it a name reflecting the baby steps I needed to painstakingly march, often stumbling, in order to recover. Every day I wrote down "one good thing" in the hope that I would read my own words as gospel and have the will to overcome the demons. My passion, the blog, became www.onegood thingbyjillee.com. And that passion got feedback, gratitude, and support as people, strangers, bolstered my courage and often told me their own and similar stories as well. When I realized that there were others just like me out there, with people who loved them and needed them to return to them whole, I wanted One Good Thing to become something for them to hold on to as well.

In time, I was not alone. As I healed, others healed along with me, and all of this brings me to where I am now: counting my blessings as I look ahead while I live each day gratefully with the promise of not only one good thing, but one good life.

With my siblings, 1967. Dori, the youngest,
had not been born yet.

one

Once I Thought
I Was a Mermaid

I grew up in a typical American family. Well, not that typical, because I have five siblings: two older brothers, Cole and Kevin; one older sister, Rebecca; and two younger sisters, JoAnn and Dori. I fall in the middle of the six. My husband, Dave, and I have four children, Erik, Britta, Kell, and Sten, and I think that's a lot. My hat's off to my mother every day.

When I was about two years old, my father started an electrical contracting business, and by the time I was in my young teens, it took off. Dad's company was responsible for the entire Tom Bradley International Terminal at LAX, and at one point, we even owned a private jet. We moved from a modest suburban community to a luxurious, gated community in Long Beach, California, called Bixby Hill. Everyone called it "Pillbox Hill" since so many doctors lived there with their families. Looking back, I realize that my childhood was one of privilege, and yet despite all the trappings of affluence, I was lucky enough to be raised in a very loving and functional family. My parents, Carole and Richard Warner, stood by me through everything and remain a loving and grounding influence in my life. There was never any doubt in my mind that my parents had a wonderful, if not idyllic, marriage. As a child, I looked up to it as a shining example. I always thought that every marriage was like theirs until I got older and realized that *not* every marriage was like theirs, which further impressed me with what a great relationship they had. Later on, when my husband and I went through our separation, I wondered whether some of our issues stemmed from my idealized view of my parents' marriage: Did I expect that my marriage should live up to theirs? Expectations can really bite you in the you-know-where.

It's almost embarrassing to admit that my family was so functional.

The Warner family, 1972

How many people can say that? My family always says that we put the *fun* in *dysfunctional* because we are and were, admittedly, a little quirky. But loving. Oh, so loving.

My parents both grew up in Utah—my mother in a small town called Kanosh and my dad in a small town called Fillmore—just a few miles down the road from each other. They met in high school. They weren't high school sweethearts, though—just friends who

My father as a young man, circa 1952

My parents' wedding, 1952

happened to fall in love a few years after graduation and stayed in love, as they are now in their eighties.

Watching my father, a man from such humble beginnings, catapult a dream that became such a successful company was always an inspiration to me. Maybe that's one of the reasons I have always had a drive and a need that occasionally border on a compulsion to succeed. Whether it was in my grade school Toastmasters club (a national club that addresses public speaking, communication, and leadership skills), campaigning and becoming the first female student body president of my junior high school, or choosing a career in the competitive, challenging field of broadcast journalism, I was always driven to overcome, to succeed, and to shine. As the saying goes, I wanted to be a planet, not just a star. Some could argue that my ambition was the result of being

My mother, circa 1950

a middle child and feeling a need to make myself more noticed. I do believe there is something to that. Perhaps it was my birth order in addition to God-given personality. Although I was hardly the forgotten one in the middle who felt as though she was caught in the shuffle. I got plenty of attention as a child. On the other hand, perhaps any one of six, regardless of the attention paid, feels a need to stand out in a crowd.

My mom was always very nurturing. For example, as a small child, I loved to write. That passion started early on. Creative writing was my favorite subject in school. Once, I wrote a story about "A Day in the Life of a Piece of Chewing Gum" that my mom still talks about to this day. In my sixth-grade class, in Toastmasters, I loved to write stories and then read them to the class. I guess you could say I was sowing the seeds of my broadcast journalism career early on. My mother always read my stories, praised them, and then posted them on the refrigerator. She was always so proud of me. She made me feel like I was the best writer on the face of the earth.

In addition to writing, there was a need in me to perform from a young age. When I became a broadcaster after graduating from Brigham Young University, that need was fulfilled. Although I left that career when motherhood called, as I write my blog and this book, I feel that my life is still a performance in a way. I'm putting myself out there. I may not be tap-dancing (although I did try that and loved it), but I am still on a stage of sorts. When I got to BYU, I considered a major in theater arts until I quickly realized that I didn't quite blend in with the theater arts group. That was when I changed my major to journalism.

From the beginning, as far back as I can remember, it was my mother who supported each and every one of my dreams and aspirations. With her guidance and support, I reached for the stars. She always encouraged my creative side, not only when it came to writing, but with so many other things as well. She was also a big advocate of instilling confidence in her children and letting us know that we could do anything if we really wanted to. All we had to do was try.

ENCOURAGING CREATIVITY IN KIDS

With today's hectic schedules, it doesn't seem like there's a lot of time for playing or just being silly. The most important thing you can do to en-

courage creativity in your kids is to give them the time to be creative—
to simply play, dream, and be, to say and do silly things. Don't schedule
every minute of every day, with things to keep them "busy." Scheduling
well-thought-out time encourages creativity and creates memories that
will last a lifetime. I can still remember spending hour after hour with
my neighborhood friend playing dolls and pretending we were "snowed
in" with our babies. Consider what imagination that took, since we lived
in sunny Southern California!

Read Books

You can encourage your kids to read if they see *you* reach for a book when
you just want to relax and unwind for a while. Children model their own
behavior on ours. Inspire your kids to get lost in books for hours on end
if they want. I can remember summers spent reading hour after hour
when I had found a particularly engaging book. I always looked forward to the summer reading program at the library. Your local library is
a treasure trove of not only books but ways to help kids love books and
become lifelong readers. Some of my favorites were:

> *The Secret Garden* by Frances Hodgson Burnett
> The Boxcar Children series by Gertrude Chandler Warner
> *James and the Giant Peach* by Roald Dahl
> *Little Women* by Louisa May Alcott

Keep Kid-Friendly Art Supplies on Hand and in Reach

First of all, don't worry if somehow the crayon gets on the wall instead
of the paper. Tips for getting it off are posted on my website. If weather
permits, take the art projects outdoors. How about drawing a family

portrait, making hand puppets from paper bags, drawing one of their dreams, a vacation they want to take, their favorite food?

Join in the Fun

Take some time out of your chores to sit down and, with colorful and thick pieces of chalk, make a fancy sidewalk drawing with your kids. They will be most impressed. Or take a trip to the local thrift store and stock up on some dress-up clothes: hats, gloves, purses, jewelry . . . the "fancier," the better. And enjoy a fancy ladies-only tea party. For the boys, my sons loved picking up miniature Hot Wheels cars at the thrift store, coming back home with their "finds," and making elaborate garages and tracks for their cars using cardboard boxes and duct tape. Doesn't that sound fun? Or make a "store" with an old cardboard box and the "food" out of old boxes from your pantry. The ideas are endless and inexpensive. The keys to raising creative kids are joining in the fun and being a role model.

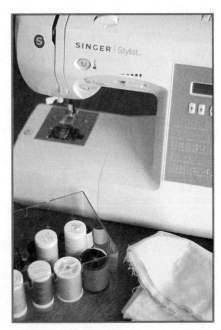

If I had to pinpoint one of my earliest childhood memories, it would be that of my mother sewing. For sure, my mother could be described as Susie Homemaker. But, if my peers in home economics class were any indication, by the time I came of age in the 1970s, sewing was nearly a lost art. My mother grew up during the Depression and watched her own mother sew the clothing for her children. And even though my mother didn't *have* to sew our clothes, particularly after my father became so successful, it was something that she wasn't giving up and encouraged us to learn. I can still sew, and it's a skill that I'm grateful for. There is something about the art of mending, repairing a seam, or merely fastening a button that is satisfying. Unless they are professional dressmakers, seamstresses, or tailors, most people I know can't repair the smallest rip in a seam. They'll sooner just throw the garment away. I distinctly remember when I was taking home economics in school (while the boys were in woodshop—those were the days!) and our assignment was to make some sort of garment. Remember the rage of those dresses with attached hoods? While the other girls were struggling with the sewing machine, needles, and thread, I made a dress that was not only hooded (a large feat in itself given the intricacy of the work) but lined as well. I must say, it was pretty amazing. And there are few things as satisfying as mastering the arts of our grandmothers and keeping them alive.

REVIVING THE ART OF SEWING AND MENDING

The ability to sew on a missing button, patch your favorite pair of jeans, or hem a thrift-store skirt is most rewarding. Mending your own clothes is not only good for the soul because it connects us with a simpler time and inspires creativity; it also saves money as we repair our clothing rather than toss perfectly good pieces or spend money to have someone else fix them for us. And don't worry, you don't have to be an expert seamstress just to sew. However, you will need to assemble a few simple essentials for your kit:

- **Needles:** Look for a pack of needles that comes with a nice assortment of different sizes for a variety of projects.
- **Thread:** Stock up on the basic colors of thread, including black, white, beige, and navy. You may also want to pick up some smaller spools of different colors, depending on your sewing needs. Prepackaged spools of thread come in a variety of colors and are fairly inexpensive. You can find them at superstores like Walmart, Target, and Kohl's, your local dollar store, and even at the supermarket in the laundry aisle.
- **Scissors:** You want a good-quality pair of scissors specifically designed for cutting fabric. These scissors should be used only for cutting fabric and should be off-limits for cutting anything else. This will help them stay sharp.
- **Straight pins:** Pins hold hems and seams in place as you repair and alter clothing. I like the ones with the colored balls on the top called dressmaker pins. They're easier to grab and hold on to and easier to spot when you inevitably drop them on the floor.

These are the essentials you'll need for a sewing basket. There are many other items, however, that are useful and handy, such as a cloth tape measure, buttons, snaps, hook and eyes, and various other types of fasteners. Other good additions would be Velcro, a white pencil for marking dark fabric, and a thimble.

The sewing basket itself doesn't have to be complicated. Find a portable container that's easy to tote to your favorite comfy chair, stock it with basic sewing essentials, and you will be well on your way to being able to tackle most of your mending and sewing needs. Breathe in the soothing power of this newly found lost art!

. . .

EVEN THOUGH there were six of us kids, we all got alone time with
our parents. Having alone time with my mom was easier since she was
at home. Having alone time with my dad was far more rare and extraordinarily special since he worked so much. Still, he managed to
carve out special times for us. One of my favorite "alone time" memories with my dad was just the two of us going to a Dodgers game. It was
a treat for my twelfth birthday. I remember that he drove like a maniac
to the stadium. At least, that was my perception. Perhaps I was simply
accustomed to driving with my mom. It was unheard of that my dad
and I would go alone to a game, and I was on cloud nine eating those
Dodger Dogs as we sat and watched the game. We also went to daddy-
daughter dates at church socials. We'd get all dressed up: I'd wear a
party dress and he'd wear a jacket and tie. All of us girls went to those
with our father, because you did it by age group. Those are memorable
nights as I recall dancing with my father.

As for my mother, despite the fact that she was at home taking care
of the six of us who were born in the proverbial stair steps, we also
managed to carve out alone time. As terrible as it was when I was diagnosed with a painful yet benign tumor in my foot, somehow my mother
turned the experience into one of the silver-lining variety. She had to
drive me to the radiation treatments, which were at the orthopedic hospital an hour from our home in Long Beach, and the treatments were
over a sixteen-week period, much of which fell during the summer. Not
a great time for a sixteen-year-old girl, whether it was summer or not.
Of course, it was always summer in Southern California, but while my
friends were enjoying the break from school, I was undergoing radiation. We turned the drive into our own private book club. I read aloud

while Mom drove. My favorite read was *Little Women* by Louisa May Alcott. With all that I was going through with my foot, those back-and-forth trips still evoke sweet memories. Whether you have an only child or a dozen, making time that's one-on-one is essential. Even just fifteen minutes can be better than nothing at all.

"DATING" YOUR KIDS

As parents, we want only the best for our kids. We cook them healthy meals, keep a clean house, enroll them in opportunities to play sports and learn a musical instrument, and so on. But sometimes we forget that what is best for our kids, and what they want the most, is our time. If you have more than one child it's important to carve out one-on-one time. With today's busy schedules it might seem impossible, but here are some tips for planning a "date night" with your kids.

Plan Ahead

Schedule dates well in advance. A little forethought will help build anticipation and help busy moms and dads stay committed to keeping the date.

Focus on the Child

If you really want to create a positive "date night," do things that truly interest your child. Plan activities that will appeal to each individual child's current interests and future aspirations.

Variety

Don't make every "date night" a dinner out. Spice things up by checking out the entertainment section of the local newspaper to see what's going on at your community center, library, or other venue. There are high school plays, sporting events, farmers' markets, tag sales, garage sales, local community service projects . . . Really, the possibilities are endless.

Keep It Interactive

Even if "date night" is a movie, try to end the evening by taking a walk or getting an ice cream cone so you can have some time to talk. Talk about anything and everything. Ask your kids about their interests, opinions, and feelings. Ask open-ended questions that can't be answered with just a yes or no.

Display Affection

All kids, even teenagers, need affection from their parents. Be sure to offer your kids genuine affection through loving words, affirmation, encouragement, small gifts, and lots of big bear hugs!

A Few Creative Date Ideas

Fly kites

Go on a hike and take pictures

Play a favorite board game

Tour a local museum or historic site

Attend a local high school play

Go to a sporting event

Visit the local zoo

Assemble a jigsaw puzzle

Go on a horseback ride

Attend a star-gazing event at a local planetarium

And, as I said before, "date nights" don't have to be complicated, and even fifteen minutes is better than nothing. They can be as simple as taking your child out to get an ice cream cone or kicking a soccer ball around in the yard. These simple one-on-one activities with your kids will have a huge effect on the quality of your relationship—now and in the future. Make the time to "date your kids" and see how good it feels.

One would think that coming from such a large family would make me crave solitude. In fact, it was always the opposite for me. I always had lots of friends and I was exceedingly social—something that became a sticking point in my marriage later on because my husband is quite the opposite. (More to come on that later.) I loved spending days at the beach, the mall, roller-skating, bike riding, and just keeping busy and active. I must say that one of the best things for me today has been the advent of Facebook. I simply love rediscovering all of my old friends as well as developing old acquaintances into new friendships. I guess it's true that certain aspects of us don't change, and socializing is still so important to me whether it's in person or electronically.

I had my first boyfriend when I was in the sixth grade and one special boyfriend in high school who was semi-serious, though not of the sweetheart variety. I loved the dances and the football games and the rallies. It was a very all-American California type of scene in Long Beach. I loved school as well and I probably would have been a better student if my social life wasn't the top priority.

All in all, my childhood was pretty wonderful. It's almost embarrassing to admit. For sure, I can't blame my parents or my upbringing for what happened to me later on in my life. My childhood was the kind that fairy tales are made of. Even our birthday parties were magical: Even though my mom had to give a lot of birthday parties for us six kids, she wanted to make sure that each one was memorable and made the birthday kid feel special.

One of my favorites was what my mom called the Mixed-Up Menu Birthday Party. It was basically a dinner party (in the middle of the day). The guests arrived and sat down at the table and were given menus with a three-course meal. But there was a catch: The menu selections didn't really describe what the food would be. The selections had crazy names, so no one really knew what they were ordering. For example, fruit punch was "Nectar of the Gods," a green salad was "Bunny Brunch," spaghetti was "Crazy Curls," ice cream was "Freeze Frame," cake was "Crummy Yummy." It was such fun! Of course, in the end, if you didn't like your menu selection, you could always choose another.

Sten participating in the
Birthday Treasure Hunt

The Mixed-Up Menu wasn't the only unusual aspect of our birthday celebrations. Really, with six kids, it was tricky to make everyone's birthday really stand out, so we always had the Birthday Treasure Hunt. We didn't just wake up in the morning and get a pile of presents and after a few minutes of tearing open boxes and paper it was all over. The Birthday Treasure Hunt was an honored family tradition that continued until I left for college (and my little sisters were still treasure-hunting while I was away from home). It's one that I have continued with my own children. Growing up in Southern California made it easy to have the hunt indoors *and* outdoors. Even though we live in Utah now, even my two kids who are born in the cold month of April have both indoor and outdoor treasure hunts. There's just something about the great outdoors. We all bundle up and off we go.

THE BIRTHDAY TREASURE HUNT

The Birthday Treasure Hunt starts with a sign in the birthday kid's room, placed on tiptoe as the child slept, so that first thing in the morning they see: *Happy Birthday, (name of birthday kid)! Let's Go on a Birthday Treasure Hunt!*

Poster board or a large piece of paper works well for this sign, along with multicolored thick markers for color, some stickers, and if you're not concerned about vacuuming post-hunt, there's always glitter to make things really sparkle.

The greeting sign is just the beginning. After the exclamatory sign, the birthday boy or girl sees a note taped to the inside of the bedroom door that might say, *Happy Birthday! Ready for your Birthday Treasure Hunt? Let's start by looking in the bathroom.* Then a note taped to the outside of the medicine cabinet or bathroom mirror reads something like, *Grab your toothbrush and rinsing cup,* and inside the cup or tied to the toothbrush is a note that might read, *Nope! Nothing here! Let's keep looking! How about the washing machine?* At the washing machine, a sign says, *Open me,* and there inside is yet another note that says, *Okay. Now it's time to have some juice!* The child heads to the fridge and there beside the juice is another clue that says, *Nope! Nothing here, but have your juice and then check out the bread box.* Tired yet? This goes on until the final destination is reached and the treasure of presents is discovered with everything but a drum roll. Even a particularly big present, like a bike, can still be found in an unusual place—like in the bathtub behind the shower curtain among other small gifts. For me as a kid and teen and for my own kids, it was like finding that pot of gold at the end of a rainbow.

Happy Birthday Hunting!

Last but not least when it comes to birthdays, there is always the cake. I am not talking about the garden-variety chocolate cake or white-frosted devil's food cake. And I am not talking about bakery cakes, either. I am talking about my mom's homemade pineapple cake. The recipe was handed down from my grandmother to my mother, and we all just loved it. That was the birthday cake that we all wanted. As a matter of fact, that was the cake that we had on any special occasion— whenever my siblings and I had a choice of dessert, we always asked for my mom's Pineapple Dessert. I asked for that cake a lot.

Even my brother Kevin, who hated all things fruit, loved that cake. Although my mom's chocolate cake with seven-minute frosting was hard to beat and totally delicious, that Pineapple Dessert was the absolute best. I don't really know how to describe it . . . It's not really a cake and it's not really a cobbler or a crumble . . . It's simply Pineapple Dessert. To this day, I would rather have that than any kind of cake in the world. I guess you're just going to have to make it and try it for yourself.

· *mom's pineapple dessert* ·

1 heaping cup powdered sugar

2 eggs, beaten

½ cup (1 stick) melted butter

1 11-ounce package vanilla wafers

1 20-ounce can crushed pineapple, drained

2 cups whipped cream (or nondairy whipped topping)

With a hand mixer or whisk, beat together the powdered sugar, eggs, and melted butter. Put the vanilla wafers in a large plastic resealable bag and crush them with a rolling pin. Pour half of the crushed wafers into the bottom of a 9 x 13 pan. Pour the egg mixture on top of the wafers, then layer on the crushed pineapple and the whipped cream. If you're using fresh whipped cream, sweeten it with a little powdered sugar. Sprinkle the rest of the crushed wafers on top. Refrigerate for a few hours before serving. Enjoy!

> *Note:* Since the eggs in this dessert are uncooked, I use pasteurized eggs for this recipe.

MAYBE ONE REASON I have been able to always make lemonade when life has given me lemons is that we had lemon trees in our backyard when I was growing up. In California, they are not really trees; they're actually more like bushes, but we called them trees. You know how growing up I thought that every marriage was perfect like my parents'? Well, I also grew up thinking that *everyone* had lemon trees in their backyards.

Whenever I needed lemon juice, I just grabbed a lemon from our tree. When I was older and had to go to the store, I thought, *Wait a second. Why am I buying lemons in a store? How come there are no lemon trees in the backyard?* When I was a kid, everyone I knew had some sort of citrus fruit in their backyard. I made tons of lemonade and had lemonade stands along with all the kids in the neighborhood. Our house was on a cul-de-sac, and it was just an idyllic place to live because we could have our lemonade stands and ride our bikes and roller-skate and we didn't have to worry about strangers or cars. It was heaven. Like living in our own playground. We simply had no worries.

Every Fourth of July we had a block party, and the neighborhood— kids and grown-ups—would get dressed up in red, white, and blue. We'd put red, white, and blue streamers on our bikes and we'd all go pool-hopping because everyone in Pillbox Hill had a pool. And there would be different foods at everyone's house—barbecues and soft drinks. The air smelled so good and clean and flavored with hickory. And wafting through the hickory coming from the barbecues was the smell of sweet citrus. Now that I live in Utah, which isn't citrus country, I thought to myself, why not . . .

GROW CITRUS INDOORS!

Those of us who don't live in a warm, sunny clime (or who live in an apartment without a backyard) can still enjoy fresh fruit picked right off the tree by growing our own citrus trees indoors. The most popular indoor fruit tree is the Meyer lemon tree. Its beautiful white blossoms act as a natural air freshener, it yields several pounds of full-size lemons every year, and trust me, once you taste fruit from your very own tree, you'll never want to buy fruit from the store again.

How to Grow Your Own Indoor Citrus Tree

Buy Right

Make sure you buy the right type of tree from the right place. Meyer lemon, kaffir lime, and calamondin oranges are all dwarf varieties that can be grown indoors. Buy from a reputable nursery to avoid diseased or inferior plants.

Pot That Plant

When you get your tree home, you will want to put it in a pot slightly larger than the root ball, with several holes for drainage in the bottom. Well-drained soil is essential for healthy citrus trees, as is soil that is slightly acidic (a pH range of 6 to 7 is best). I would highly suggest buying a premixed potting soil formulated specifically for citrus.

A Sunny Space

Citrus should ideally get ten to twelve hours of sunlight a day, although six to eight hours is usually sufficient. Place plants by a south-facing window with good airflow and, if necessary, supplement the sun with grow lights during darker months. If you want, you can put your tree outdoors on a sunny patio or balcony in the warmer months, but it isn't a requirement.

Avoid a Chill

Citrus trees are happiest when temperatures stay between 55 and 85 degrees, and they dislike abrupt temperature change, so be sure to keep them away from chilly drafts and heater vents.

Keep It Moist

Regular watering is key to your citrus tree's survival, but water just enough so the soil is on the dry side of moist. These trees do not like to sit in a puddle of water. They also crave humidity (think Florida), so mist with water regularly and, if necessary, position near a humidifier.

Pollinate to Produce

To get citrus trees to reliably set fruit indoors, where no bees are buzzing around, you can hand-pollinate using a small paintbrush. Collect the yellow pollen from the tips of the feathery anthers inside a flower, and then brush the pollen against the sticky surface of the stigma in the center of a blossom. Repeat with each flower.

Reap the Harvest

The time from blossom to harvesting your fruit varies. In general, most lemons and limes will ripen in six to nine months, and oranges will be ready to harvest in about a year.

Soon enough, you will be harvesting your lemons, limes, and oranges and making desserts (and other yummy stuff) that will make you feel like you're in sunny California even if it's snowing outside.

LOOKING BACK on my childhood wouldn't be complete without the imagery of the beach. You just can't escape the beach culture when you grow up in California, and I was the quintessential California girl—

My dad at a beach party, 1987

Dave and our nephew
Danny at a beach party

and even though I never mastered the art of getting up on a surfboard, I was still a surfer girl. I also never mastered the art of getting up on water skis. Now, bodyboarding was another story—that's where I excelled.

When I was a teenager and especially when school was out, I spent a lot of time hanging out at the beach with my friends. I was part of the "popular" group. There were pool parties and sleepovers when I was younger, but once I started high school, even though my peers were still hanging out at the beach, things changed for me. A lot of my friends were partying hard—which included not only drinking (I was a late bloomer, I say tongue in cheek) but having sex—and I bowed out. That scene was just not for me. My family belonged to the Church of Jesus Christ of Latter-day Saints (LDS), and that sort of behavior defied my belief system.

But that didn't stop the family parties at the beach. We bought one of those big galvanized trash cans and filled it with fresh seawater and put in tons of ears of corn. We roasted it over a fire pit until the corn was done, and that was just so incredibly delicious. Then we'd roast hot dogs and marshmallows over the fire, and it was just amazing. And the swimming. I have always loved to swim. I think I spent more time under the water than on top. Every summer I had swimmer's ear, which drove my mother crazy. For me, it was another world under the sea. My favorite make-believe was pretending that I was a mermaid.

THROWING THE ULTIMATE BEACH PARTY!

By now you know that one of my very favorite things about growing up in Southern California was the beach. I loved the sun, the sand, the waves, the cheese fries from the snack bar . . . but most of all, I loved the beach parties. Sometimes they were just our family, sometimes friends, but regardless of the guest list, the basic recipe was always the same.

It would start out with a fifty-gallon galvanized steel trash can and several dozen ears of fresh corn. About an hour before the beach party was scheduled to begin, at least two individuals would start the fire at the designated fire ring and then go fill the trash can with seawater. (You needed *two* people because that

Our nephew Nathan
enjoying his cake

thing was *heavy* after being filled with seawater!) The can would be placed on the fire and loaded up with the corn. Once the corn was done and the party guests had arrived . . . the party began.

Other Required Ingredients for the Ultimate Beach Party

> Plenty of chairs for sitting around the fire
>
> Hot dogs and all the fixins
>
> All the fixins for s'mores
>
> Lots of roasting sticks (which were more often than not
>   straightened-out wire hangers)

Lots of butter and salt for the fresh corn on the cob

Cans of soda in big buckets of ice

LOTS OF NAPKINS!

As evening set in, the bravest (or most foolhardy) among us would take a dip in the water during the party, and some of the brazen "lovebirds" might sneak off to a lifeguard tower for a quick smooch (or ten), but for the most part we all bundled up in warm sweatshirts and sat around the fire eating, laughing, and generally having the time of our lives. We would all end up going home smelling like smoke, sticky from marshmallows, and covered in sand, but in my opinion, there was no greater feeling.

Whether I was pretending to be a mermaid or simply daydreaming, I always had what I call a "rich inner life." Some people called it an overactive imagination. I often pretended that my life was a movie and I would wonder, *What scene should we be filming now?* I wondered about everything. There was always a story in everything for me. Even when I walked to school or around the neighborhood, I wondered as I wandered. There was a set of condos that I passed each day when I walked to school, and in the early morning, their shades were often drawn and I'd make up stories as to what was happening inside. I observed everything and made up stories in my head. The olfactory sense is powerful, and I remember how I always thought I smelled scalloped potatoes as I walked past those condos. Scalloped potatoes in the morning? To this day, I love the smell of scalloped potatoes.

Lemons, scalloped potatoes, corn on the cob roasting in seawater, mermaids, and treasure hunts. A childhood just doesn't get better than the one I had. I strive to do the same for my children. When I think about what I went through as an adult, I think it's just so unusual under the circumstances of my beginnings. Someone else could blame their childhood. I can't. I cannot place blame on anyone but myself. I take full responsibility for my bad decisions, but onwards and upwards I go because, at the end of the day, I am blessed to be one of the lucky ones.

two

I Left My Heart in California, but Found It in Bismarck

I n 1980, I headed off to Brigham Young University in Provo, Utah. Seven hundred miles and a good ten-hour drive (at least) from home. There were several reasons why I really didn't consider other colleges. I'd always wanted to go to BYU because my brothers and sister went there and my family had always been big fans of their sports teams. Two of my closest friends were going to attend BYU, and it's a Latter-day Saints college. What I didn't comprehend at the time was that although my family went to church every Sunday, I still grew up in a community that was not predominantly LDS. When I got to college, and later on when I moved to Utah with my husband and children, I found the Mormon culture to be overwhelming. Growing up in a Latter-day Saints family was simply who we were. BYU was truly in my comfort zone.

Mom and I went clothes shopping before I left for school, and for sure, the focus was on cold-weather clothing: gloves, hats, scarves, boots, and a winter coat. My family was a huge skiing family, and we took yearly ski trips to Alta and Snowbird in Utah and to Mammoth in California, so I wasn't exactly a stranger to cold weather, but living in a cold climate was another story entirely. My wardrobe changed substantially.

A family ski trip, circa 1977. My sister Rebecca is on the left,
JoAnn is in the center, and I'm on the right.

My friend Terri and I planned to make the drive to BYU into a mini road trip. I was really excited until the night before, when the prospect of leaving home hit me. I was in my room, crying as I tried to sort out the mixture of fear and excitement . . . but fear was winning out. My dad came into my room and asked if it would make me feel better if I had a new car for the trip and to keep at school. I remember blubbering "yes" through sobs.

The next morning, we packed up my new Mazda RX-7. It was just my stuff because Terri had the foresight to ship hers ahead. Thank goodness, because that car was packed to the hilt. There were my clothes—tons of clothes—books, stereo (back in the day when we had those big stereos and speakers), CDs, toiletries, and, of course, my beloved electric typewriter. My mom and dad were in the driveway along with my younger sisters, and just as Terri and I were about to leave, I started bawling again. My parents were crying, too. Even my tough-businessman dad was all choked up, because when it came to his kids—especially his daughters—he had a huge soft spot. I have never been good with good-byes. I can't even watch good-byes on TV. I just start to weep. That good-bye was one of the toughest, but once Terri and I got on the road, I was okay.

Terri and I switched off driving, played the radio and CDs (a lot of Chicago, Boston, and Bread), and talked about what lay ahead. To this day, whenever I hear a Bread song, I think of that drive. Years later, Terri named one of her daughters Aubrey, after the Bread song. We stopped here and there to get a snack or use a restroom, but we drove straight through, skimming the corner of Arizona, through Nevada, and then into Utah, where we arrived on campus.

At least an unfamiliar roommate wasn't a factor. I was rooming with one of my other close friends, Diana, and eliminating that unknown helped a lot. We carried all of our stuff, hiking the three floors to our dorm room, and suddenly it all became very exciting. That tiny little room was my "own" place—the first one I had where I wasn't living under the safe roof of my parents' house. Diana and I decided it would be fun to decorate, and so off we went to Pier 1 Imports, where we bought storage bins, pillows, a rug, and coverlets and made our little room into a home.

SURVIVAL TIPS FOR MOVING
(ACROSS TOWN OR ACROSS THE COUNTRY)

In the first seven years of our marriage, Dave and I moved seven times. By the seventh time, I kind of had it down to a science. Here are my tried-and-true tips for making a move as painless as possible:

Plan ahead! Start packing weeks in advance. This takes a lot of the stress out of a move. Start with the stuff you hardly ever use and then decide what out of that *will* never be used and throw that stuff out. Box up the rest and label it well—preferably on all sides with a large, black Sharpie, and be specific. Instead of *Bedroom* or *Bathroom*, take time to write out which bedroom or bathroom (if there is more than one) and a general list of contents. For example, *Hall Bathroom: towels and decorative items*, or *Master Bedroom: books, nightstand contents, etc.* This makes unpacking at your destination much easier. You don't have people who are helping you constantly asking, "Where does this box go?" and the whole process goes so much faster this way. Time is of the essence whether your labor force is paid (i.e., professional movers) or unpaid (i.e., family and friends).

Hold a garage sale. I'd say to plan this for a month before your move, so that you aren't simultaneously stressing over both the move and the sale. Get rid of everything you can think of that will not be useful to you in your new place. It's such a waste of time, energy, and resources to pack, transport, and unpack things you are just going to throw away when you get to your new place.

Use a variety of box sizes. There are different sizes for a reason. Don't pack two hundred books in a great big box. No one is going to be able to lift it. Divide and conquer those books into smaller boxes. (Your back will thank you.)

Make sure you go through your house with a fine-tooth mental comb and take everything that belongs to you. Don't forget the window covering in the garage or the hummingbird feeder in the backyard.

If you need a moving truck, reserve it at least two weeks in advance. When in doubt, reserve the size bigger than you think you need.

Make sure to pack a "survival box" containing the essentials of life, such as children's blankies or teddy bears, bedsheets, blankets and pillows, an alarm clock, etc. Tape it up with neon-colored duct tape or plaster it with big stickers, anything that makes it stand out like a sore thumb, and put it in the truck last so it's first out in your new place.

Despite the new decor, the first night in the dorm was bittersweet. I was excited, nervous about starting school, and though I tried not to be, I was still homesick. Being with Diana and Terri made it better, but I missed my family and all the comforts of home. I even missed just saying good night to my parents. It wasn't lost on me that this was my first time away from home. I never went to sleepaway camp like a lot of other kids. Going away to college was a huge step for me.

At first, I thought that I wanted to major in theater arts. Singing and acting tapped in to the performer in me. I always had a fascination and love for New York City and even dreamed that someday Broadway might beckon. But once I started taking the theater classes at BYU, I felt that I didn't fit in. I wanted to be on the stage, but it seemed to me that the other students in my theater classes were *always* on stage. I enjoyed drama, but I didn't *live* dramatically. We even dressed differently: My demeanor and attire were more "of the time"—shoulder pads and oversize shirts; their attire was more avant-garde and bohemian. It didn't take me long to discover that the theater scene at BYU was quite different from the high school production crowd back home. In short, it just wasn't me.

When I realized that I didn't blend with the theater crowd, I decided to try a journalism course, since English and writing were my other loves. Once I took Journalism 101, I was smitten. It spoke to my innate curiosity about the world. There were those five essential *W*s—who, what, where, when, and why—that had to be addressed in the lead of any article that gave me license to go out there and ask all the questions I wanted to. As a journalist I had the perfect right: I was getting the scoop and not just being a snoop. I'd never thought about the broadcast aspect of journalism until I took that 101 class, which was taught by a man named Lynn Packer. Mr. Packer was in his forties, and although I really was interested in journalism, I confess that I was also infatuated with Mr. Packer. He was just so cute—and yes, he also was a charismatic teacher. He was a real "crusty" reporter, a true investigative journalist as well as a broadcaster. I was just crazy about him, along with every other girl in Journalism 101. Between Mr. Packer's class and the broadcasting classes where we went out with the camera, shot "news stories," and then edited the videotapes, I was hooked. I wanted to be a reporter and an anchor. I was comfortable in front of the camera, and that's where my desire to perform came in handy. It all came together. I found my stage that was steeped more in reality than drama and satisfied my love of storytelling and natural curiosity: the perfect blend.

Graduating from college with a degree in broadcast journalism basically leaves you with two choices. You can look for a job where you will be a small fish in a big pond, or vice versa. Knowing my desire to shine, I bet it's not hard to figure out which choice I made. Yes, I chose the latter, because I didn't graduate with a major in broadcast journalism to go sit at an assignment desk in a big city. I wanted to be in front of the camera. Right after graduation, I went with a group of BYU students to New York City, where we all had unpaid internships at different types of companies. I had two internships—one at ABC News and another at CNN, which was located in the lobby of the World Trade Center.

I had never been to New York City before, and we were all staying in the dorms at Columbia Teachers College. My room was so tiny, just enough room for a bed, really. And it was hot and there was no air-conditioning. For those of you who don't know New York City, my dorm was at the northern end of the island of Manhattan, and CNN was at the southernmost point. Talk about getting to know my way around.

Everything about that internship was such a great experience. I worked on the assignment desk at CNN during the era of Mary Alice Williams, who was one of my idols. I often arranged travel and accommodations for her guests. One of the guests was the unforgettable Bella Abzug. That internship fueled my drive to succeed in the biz even more.

In addition to what I learned professionally during that eight-week stint, I also learned how to dress differently. I wasn't a college kid or a California girl anymore. I had to dress the part, and even though I brought only a few outfits with me, I had to make them work.

DRESSING FOR SUCCESS

If you look good, you feel good. For me, that's the most important aspect of "dressing for success." This can be applied whether you're attending school, working in an office, or even working from home. Even if you don't have to impress anyone, you will still benefit, in terms of confidence and self-esteem, if you give time and attention to the way you dress. Bottom line: Although I don't always practice what I preach, I try not to work from home in my pajamas or sweatpants. Here I give you my favorite tried-and-true "dressing for success" rules.

Buy the Best Quality You Can Afford

It's better to invest in a few good pieces than to purchase a lot of disposable clothes. Good fabric is key. It looks better and lasts longer, and holds its shape better.

Develop Your Own Style

Whatever your business is, you need to create a look for yourself that people remember and that speaks to your personality and individuality.

Leave the Bar Attire at the Bar

In my opinion, wearing sexy attire in the workplace puts women into the "less competent" category. It doesn't matter how smart you are—if you wear a décolleté neckline and a miniskirt, people—men and women—will not take you seriously.

Dress for Your Figure

Learn about your specific body type and what styles enhance your best features. It's not about size; it's about shape, proportion, and balance. Embrace your body shape, don't fight it.

Ask for Help

If you don't have the first clue as to how to go about building a professional wardrobe, go to a large department store and request a personal shopper. They're trained to help you choose items that best fit your career, body type, and lifestyle. Typically, personal shoppers are available at no extra charge. Also, many salespeople will help with selections. You just have to ask.

The Rule of Three

When considering a clothing purchase, be sure each piece passes the rule of three: Can you think of three things to wear it with, three places to wear it, and three ways to accessorize it?

It's Always Better to Be Overdressed Than Underdressed

This is a good general rule for professional situations as well as social ones. For example, it's better to wear casual slacks on dress-down Fridays than blue jeans.

Your Iron Is Your Friend

Enough said.

Don't Over-Accessorize

Less is always more.

Wear Subtle Perfumes for Work

You want people to catch just a slight scent and not be overwhelmed by a bouquet of gardenia.

Proper Undergarments Are a Must

Take the time to find pieces that work with your body and your budget. Check out Target's ASSETS line (a lower-cost line by the makers of Spanx) and, ladies, watch those panty lines!

No Chipped Nail Polish

And better to have short, well-groomed nails and cuticles than long nails if the maintenance is too time-consuming and/or costly. Clear or sheer nail polishes hold up longer and chips don't show.

Pay Attention to Your Glasses, Both Prescription and Sunglasses

Make sure they fit your face.

Wear Comfortable and Well-Maintained Shoes

Nothing ruins a look more than scuffed shoes with the heels worn down or Band-Aids covering blisters. Ouch!

Remember Your Breath

Keep it fresh. Carry mints or breath strips in your pocket or purse.

Three Things to Keep at Work for Fashion Emergencies

Stain remover pen, lint roller, and safety pins. And if you can sew, add a fourth: a pocket-size sewing kit for those times when you lose a button or your hem comes down.

Always Wear a Smile

You're never fully dressed without a smile.

THE SUMMER AFTER COLLEGE I worked as my dad's receptionist for some pocket money after my internship in New York ended. While there I sent out résumés and audition tapes from my broadcast journalism classes that showed my anchor experience. BYU really helps their graduates with job placement, and because they also have such an illustrious broadcast journalism program, I soon found a job. After a few months at my dad's office, on a late fall day, I got a call from Darrell Dorgan, the news director at KXMB-TV in Bismarck, North Dakota, who said I was hired.

Over the next month, as I packed my bags, I never considered what a huge step this was. Not only was I moving halfway across the country, I was heading out on my very own for the very first time. This wasn't the same as being in college, when I came home for summers and holidays. I was moving from warm, sunny California to the frozen tundra of North Dakota in the middle of winter. But I was superexcited at the prospect of starting my career. The notion that Bismarck would be even colder than Provo escaped me. The idea that I didn't know a soul in Bismarck also didn't play into my thoughts.

My dad and I flew to Bismarck the day after Christmas 1985. I had many suitcases with clothing (those were the days when airlines didn't charge for extra baggage), and this time we were smart enough to ship my books, typewriter, and CDs ahead of time. When we landed in North Dakota, it was the definition of the dead of winter. It was bitterly cold and so windy that the snow was coming down horizontally. We checked in to a hotel and then went apartment hunting. We found an efficiency apartment—a furnished one-room with a kitchen that was really more like a counter. The two of us went out and bought sheets, towels, pillows, pots and pans, a small set of dishes, and some grocery staples that were just enough to keep me alive. Who knew that cereal would be the mainstay of my diet on so many nights?

NEW APARTMENT ESSENTIALS

Basic Furniture
Bed

Pillows and bedding

Dresser

Nightstand

Couch and chair(s)

Coffee table

Bookshelves

TV and/or entertainment stand

Dining table and chairs

Bathroom Supplies
Shower curtain, bath mat, and bath rug

Toilet paper

Towels and washcloths

Wastebasket

Toiletries

Basic first-aid kit

Bar soap

Body wash

Shampoo

Conditioner

Moisturizer

Rubbing alcohol

Hydrogen peroxide

Kitchen Supplies

Two saucepans, one small and one large

Two skillets, one small and one large

Cookie sheet

9 x 13 baking pan

Potholders

Dry and liquid measuring cups

Utensils, including a wooden spoon, whisk, spatula, tongs, and a
    large slotted spoon

Two knives, one large and one paring

Cutting board

Cheese grater

Ice cream scoop

Large serving bowl that can be used for salad or pasta

Flatware

Dishes: plates, bowls, cups, glassware

Napkins

Dish soap

Sponges

Dish towels and paper towels

Aluminum foil and plastic wrap

Trash can

Basic seasonings and dried spices

Basic condiments—jam, honey, ketchup, mustard, mayonnaise, hot
   sauce, taco sauce

Cookbooks (and some of Mom's easy and best recipes)

A small fire extinguisher

Laundry and Cleaning Basics

Rags

Sponges

Mop

Bucket

All-surface polish

Toilet scrub brush

Garbage bags

Vacuum cleaner or electric broom

Broom and dustpan

Laundry detergent

Laundry bag or basket

Stain remover

After Dad took me shopping for the essentials, he bought me a new car. It was my belated graduation present, and I needed something to brave the brutal North Dakota winters. We chose an all-wheel drive gray Honda Accord. While there, the dealer encouraged us to purchase a block heater. *A block heater?* It's an engine heater, because it gets so cold in Bismarck that you have to plug your car in to a block heater at night so the engine doesn't freeze. There was a parking spot for me in the single-story apartment complex where I lived and, sure enough, there was a plug next to the spot.

Finally, it was time to drive my dad to the airport, and you can't imagine the scene that ensued there. The thrill of my budding career left me momentarily as I realized that I was totally alone, starting a new job, and didn't know a soul in Bismarck. I sobbed uncontrollably. I did all but cry out "Don't leave me!" I was crying so hard that not only did my dad start to cry as we stood there hugging each other, but two little old ladies who were watching us started to cry, too.

My first day on the job was exciting and daunting, as all first days on the job are, and after it was over, all I wanted was to go home. To tell you the truth, I wanted to go home every day for the next few months. I'd call my parents and cry and say how homesick I was, and my mom always said, "Just give it six weeks. If you still feel this way in six weeks, you can come home." I was so visibly homesick that my news director later confessed that he drove by my apartment every night after his day was done just to make sure that my car was still there and I hadn't flown the coop. He and I are still in touch to this day, and this is one of his favorite stories to tell when he rings my house at Christmastime each year.

HOW TO DEAL WITH HOMESICKNESS

Keep in Touch

Things are quite different now from what they were when I was in Bismarck. Back then, there was no Skype, no FaceTime, no e-mail, and phone calls were long distance. Now, keeping in touch takes only an instant even if you're halfway across the world. My daughter recently returned from a three-week trip to Europe, and while she was there Dave and I got to talk to her via FaceTime almost every other day. There she was, in living color, in Rome and Athens, and also on my phone screen in Utah. It was surreal, but awesome. Because I was able to touch base with her, at least via technology, every few days, I didn't miss her nearly as much as I might have if I'd received only a postcard or two. Technology is there, so use it.

Make Plans to See the People You're Leaving Behind

Plan a girls' or guys' getaway for six months from the time you move. *Make* the reservations. Don't just *talk* about it (like I always did). This not only makes leaving easier ("What are you crying about? I'll see you in Hawaii in six months!") but also gives you something to look forward to when you're homesick.

Keep Busy

Whether you are moving for work, school, or both, dive right in. Get involved in your job, your community, your dorm or apartment building. My mother always advises people to "lose yourself in service." One of my favorite phrases is "activity relieves anxiety." If you're feeling anxious about being lonely, get up and do something. From personal experience, wallowing only makes it that much worse.

Feather Your Nest

I have always found comfort in unpacking and setting up all my personal possessions in order to make a house (or even a single room) a home. Favorite posters, artwork, photographs, and home decor items that connect me to the home I just left make me feel as though I belong where I am. Going shopping for just a few new items also helps you feel more settled as you put your stamp on the new place.

At the anchor desk at KXMB

Give It Time

This is most important. Moving away from home for the first time (or any time) can be formidable. As excited as you are to pursue your new adventure in life, it's hard to move to a place that is completely foreign. Don't expect to fall in love with everything the first day. It takes time to get accustomed to your new surroundings, but you will. Trust me on this one. Take it one day at a time, and pretty soon you'll have several days behind you, then several weeks, and before you know it your "new" home will become home sweet home.

IN BISMARCK, Mom's "give it six weeks" became nearly two years. Really, giving oneself time to adjust in any situation is essential. I was a weekday reporter and the weekend anchor (we had only one newscast per day on the weekend, and it wasn't quite a full half hour). I should qualify this by telling you that I was the *only* weekend anchor. I did news, weather, and sports (which was kind of hilarious).

What wasn't funny was my financial situation. For the first time in my life, I had to pay my rent, electricity, phone, food, clothing, toiletries, makeup, lifestyle . . . The list goes on. I was never a great manager of money, but I didn't really overspend and I was never overly concerned (though I wish that I had been) because I knew that, if push came to shove, my dad would help me out of a bind. I have a different wisdom now as I think, *What if I hadn't had him?* I think that financial issues played a tremendous role in adding to the stress of my marriage later on. Here's the thing: Back in the day in Bismarck, I used a credit card and it didn't feel like I was spending money. Of all the wonderful things that my parents did for me, perhaps the only mistake they made was making life too easy. It wasn't until I was on my own that I realized the value of a dollar. Now, I feel that is an essential part of raising a child. Financial literacy is not taught in our schools. If our kids don't learn the value of a dollar at home, they don't learn it at all. But home is actually the best place to teach it if we want to impart our own financial values to our children. So how do we teach kids the value of a dollar in today's "buy now, pay later" world?

TEACHING YOUR KIDS
THE VALUE OF A DOLLAR

Start Early

Kids as young as six years old can begin to understand the concepts of spending, saving, and giving to charity. In fact, when you start teaching children about money and finance early in life, it simply becomes second nature to them, as opposed to something that is stressful when they become teens and young adults.

Set a Good Example

Children do as they see, not always as they are told. Pay your bills on time. Don't be afraid to say no when things don't fit into your budget (and *tell* your child it is not in the budget). Practice what you preach.

Pay Your Children a "Commission"

Assign children jobs around the house that are associated with certain dollar amounts. If they do the job, they get paid. If they don't do the job, they don't get paid. It's as simple as that.

The important thing is for children to have some money that is their own to manage, save, and spend. Accountability is a good lesson to learn, and having to take care of one's own money is a good way to learn.

Use *Spend, Save,* and *Share* Jars

This three-jar money system, with separate containers for each of your child's money goals, is a simple way to teach a child how to manage their income.

Label three separate jars with the words *Spend, Save,* and *Share.*

As your kids receive an allowance or earn money elsewhere, you decide how much money should be deposited into each jar (i.e., 50 percent into spending, 25 percent into saving, and 25 percent into sharing).

Money in the Spend jar is for trips to the toy store, or any other place your child wants.

Money in the Save jar can be placed into savings at a local bank when the child has enough to open an account.

Money in the Share jar can be used for charitable donations. The family can decide on the recipients and causes together.

Using the Spend, Save, and Share jars provides great teaching moments with your kids when it comes to giving to others and spending wisely. These lessons lay a foundation for the rest of their lives. Remember, the best financial advisor your children will ever have is you. I must admit that I learned the hard way. Now, I heed advice from the experts, and these are tips that I hold dear. There are countless blogs, articles, tips, and books about how to get *out* of debt, but I personally prefer the ones that teach us how to not get into debt in the first place.

Back to the newsroom, now that I've finished my segment on Finance with Your Kids by Jillee. Really, the toughest and most hilarious part of my job came when I had to recap all the national sports highlights. I had to come up with so many synonyms as I announced the scores. Like: So-and-so *trounced* or *defeated* or *thrashed, creamed, bashed.* It was ridiculous!

As for weekly news reporting, the big stories were the ones out of Bismarck, the state capital, and there was a lot of political coverage. I covered the legislature and did every other conceivable story there was across the Midwest: housing starts, agricultural reports, oil and gas mining reports, unemployment, teen pregnancy. You name it, I probably covered it. There was never a dull moment, and that was just the way I liked it. I crisscrossed the state of North Dakota many times to unearth news reports as well as feature stories. One of my favorite trips was the time I went to Strasburg, North Dakota, population of around seven hundred people, but it *was* the birthplace of Lawrence Welk.

KXMB-TV news staff. Dave is at far left,
and I am third from the left, standing.

The most exciting news coverage, however, was always the weather. My cameraman Dave and I went out storm-chasing and then covered the aftereffects. We saw some pretty scary stuff. There were tornados right out of *The Wizard of Oz*, lightning that ignited the sky like strobe lights, and rain and wind of near-Biblical proportions. Once, we had to stop the car under a freeway overpass for fear that the car would become airborne. You've never experienced a lightning and thunderstorm until you've experienced a North Dakota storm.

Back to cameraman Dave. I was hired just after he was, and I remember the first day that I saw him walk into the newsroom. He was so cute and tall and blond and Norwegian (but grew up in Fargo), and although I was still feeling homesick, I thought, *Hmmm . . . maybe it's not so bad here in Bismarck after all.* We worked together for about a year and were just good friends, although I had a crush on him. Much later, he confessed that he had a crush on me as well. We really were just the best of friends for an entire year. We hit it off so well and we hung out a lot because we were both new to Bismarck. Our news direc-

In Bismarck before our wedding

tor used to tease us that we were romantically involved, even though we weren't. He must have had a sixth sense, though.

I remember the evening when the friendship turned. We went to Peacock Alley, the local station hangout in downtown Bismarck, and Dave drove me home. He was going to drop me off, but I invited him inside and he dimmed the lights. As we sat on the couch, he pulled the ol' yawn-stretching-out-the-arm thing. And then he leaned over and kissed me. That was the beginning, and the rest is history. We got engaged only a few months later, on Valentine's Day 1987. I had moved to a new one-bedroom apartment. It was extremely cold out, but I cooked a special Valentine's Day dinner, Chateaubriand, on my tiny little balcony on my little Weber grill. Dave got down on one knee and proposed. Four months later, we were married. In the interim, he converted to my LDS faith, in part because he knew how much it meant to me and my family.

Does anyone wonder why one of my favorite movies is *When Harry Met Sally?* Just when we finally had everyone convinced it wasn't romantic, it became romantic. To this day, our former news director takes credit for our union. Now, it may not be the best thing to date someone in the workplace, but it worked out just fine for Dave and me.

DATING SOMEONE YOU WORK WITH

Dating someone you work with may have its challenges, but for me and the hubster it worked out quite well. Even Barack and Michelle met on the job, so how bad can it be? A 2012 CareerBuilder survey revealed that of those who dated at work, 31 percent said their office romances wound up leading to marriage. That said, it still can be a delicate operation with plenty of pros and cons to consider carefully.

The Pros

- You share the same passion.
- Work gives you insight into how the other person handles daily challenges.
- If you're working together, you often have a greater sense of the person before you actually commit to dating them.
- You speak the same language. This was especially valuable working in TV, which has a language all its own.
- Your partner knows your strengths and weaknesses and can help provide honest feedback and guidance.
- When you're having a bad day at work, there is always a bright spot.

The Cons

- Breaking up is hard to do in the best of times, and having to see your ex-boyfriend or ex-girlfriend at work every day can be emotionally challenging and create an unhappy working environment.
- Your relationship may influence decisions that go well beyond a lunchroom, such as promotions, projects, and responsibilities.
- If you start a relationship with someone in your office, you can be sure that other people will gossip about it. It's inevitable and unavoidable.
- Seeing each other during workdays followed by seeing each other socially in the evenings and weekends can lead to a little *too* much togetherness.

Some Guidelines

> Keep the boundaries clear between your personal and professional lives. While on the job, your focus should be 100 percent on your responsibilities, not your romance.

> It is strongly recommended *not* to date your boss or someone who is in authority. If you really think this is the love of your life, consider leaving your job before you start a relationship.

> Be discreet. Remember to respect your work environment and the people in it.

> Maintain boundaries: Don't bring your arguments or romantic conversations to work.

> Learn the internal policies of the company before starting the relationship. Some employers strictly prohibit romantic relationships at work.

Dave and I were married on June 13, 1987, in my parents' backyard in Huntington Beach. They moved from Long Beach while I was in college. It was an absolutely beautiful home near the harbor, with an in-ground rock hot tub surrounded by a waterfall. My mother was and is an amazing gardener, and she planted pink, white, and purple impatiens everywhere as soon as I got engaged. Mom and I planned the wedding long-distance, and someone in Bismarck made my dream wedding gown of French lace. Dave wore a white tux and white bow tie. The following day, we took a helicopter to Catalina Island off the California coast and spent a week's honeymoon there before taking a boat back to Huntington Beach. It was glorious.

I must confess that as much as I loved our wedding and our honeymoon, what I really loved was how my skin felt in the warm weather as opposed to the cold air of North Dakota. But I couldn't believe how frizzy my hair was in California. I'd forgotten how tough it had been to tame. I didn't need to be calmed on my wedding day, but my hair sure did. Since Dave and I have settled in Utah for the long haul, I have learned a lot of tricks over the years to keep hair and skin looking fab, no matter what the weather. It's taken a lot of experimentation, just shy of a full-time job. Have a look at the tips and see what works best for you.

My wedding day, 1987

FIVE TIPS FOR BEAUTIFUL SKIN AND HAIR IN ANY CLIMATE

For Hot and Humid Climates

Skin Care

- Store beauty products in the fridge. That way, they always will feel cool and refreshing despite the heat.
- Put away your heavy winter moisturizer and use a lightweight water-based one instead. A lighter moisturizer will feel less sticky and will allow your skin to breathe more.

- Once a week, use an exfoliator to get rid of dead skin cells.
- Carry some tissue blotters in your purse to blot away any moisture from your face whenever you need a touch-up.
- Switch from a cream foundation to a powdered one. Powders will give you a similar effect and are much better for your skin in the humid weather.
- Always wash off makeup before bed. This is especially important because bacteria breed more in high temperatures. You have to let your skin breathe overnight, because that's when it repairs and replenishes itself. Think of sleep as detox time for your skin.
- Drink plenty of water in order to keep hydrated and cool. This is one of the best methods of regulating your body temperature and keeping both you and your skin from feeling and looking hot and bothered.
- Finally, cleanse daily with a gentle cleanser to rid the skin of impurities that build up in warmer weather. Sometimes warm and humid weather can cause acne or breakouts. Did you know that strawberries contain salicylic acid, a key ingredient in many over-the-counter acne medications? Consider a homemade facial mask made with strawberries, as described below.

· *fresh strawberry mask* ·

½ cup fresh strawberries

2 tsp honey

1 egg white

Blend all the ingredients in a blender on high speed until smooth. Spoon the mixture into a clean container with a tight-fitting lid and store it in the refrigerator. Spread over your face, neck, chest, back, and shoulders (or anywhere else you may have breakouts). Leave on for 20 minutes, and then rinse well with luke-warm water. The mixture keeps for up to a week in the refrigerator.

Hair Care

- Lather up only a few times a week. The natural oils that accumulate are good frizz fighters. If your hair feels oily, use a dry shampoo between washes.
- Don't fight Mother Nature. If your hair is naturally curly, rock your natural curls when it's humid. Not only is it easier, but being yourself will boost your confidence.
- Talk to your stylist about how to take off extra hair weight. A real pro can style you for any weather.
- To tame the frizzies, you'll need the right products. Invest in a good smoothing serum and a hydrating cream to keep hair moisturized. Let washed hair air-dry. Blow-drying often causes more frizz.
- If all else fails, hide the frizz with a pretty, loose bun.

For Cold and Dry Climates

Skin Care

- Take shorter showers and use tepid water. Hot water might feel good on a cold morning, but it strips skin of its natural oils, leaving it dehydrated and itchy.
- Use a creamy facial cleanser—the milkier, the better. Steer clear of cleansers that contain harsh detergents such as triclosan and ammonium lauryl sulfate. Check the label for gentle surfactants like sodium laureth sulfate and cocamidopropyl betaine.
- After showers or baths, apply an oil-based cream to better trap and lock moisture into skin. For better absorption, warm the jar of cream in a sink of hot water while you shower.
- Moisturize after your morning shower or bath and then again at bedtime. There's a slight elevation in body temperature while you're sleeping, so products seep into skin better. For dry hands and feet, slather on a rich cream and wear cotton gloves and socks to bed. This will prevent evaporation and help the cream penetrate better.
- Did you know that avocado provides replenishing moisture and honey helps to heal chafed and raw areas? If your skin is dry and/or peeling, consider this homemade facial mask:

· avocado and honey mask ·

½ very ripe avocado (any kind)

2 tbsp honey

½ tsp coconut oil

Mash or puree the avocado until it's smooth and creamy, and then blend in the honey and coconut oil. Apply the mixture to your face, avoiding your eyes, and leave it on for 10 to 15 minutes. Wipe your skin clean with a damp, warm cloth, or rinse your face with warm water in the shower.

Hair Care

- Shampoo only every two or three days. Daily washing depletes natural oils. Less frequent washing also avoids the use of high-heat tools like flat irons and blow-dryers.

- Wash your hair backward. First, apply half a teaspoon of your favorite oil to your scalp and work it through. You can use jojoba, olive, or sweet almond oil. Second, apply your conditioner and let it sit for a few minutes. Third, shampoo with a moisturizing formula and follow with a leave-in conditioner. With this method your hair takes the nutrients it needs from the oil and conditioner and the shampoo washes the unneeded portion out. The result is clean, shiny, healthy hair.

- Avoid using products that contain alcohol or directly spraying perfume into your hair. Alcohol will strip your hair of its natural moisture, leaving it dry and brittle.

- Wear a hat or scarf to protect your hair when out in the cold. A hat with a satin lining won't mess up your hair or cause static.

- Deep condition your hair once a week during winter months to help with moisture retention.

- Finish off showers with a cold-water rinse. A cool rinse of water will close the cuticle and seal in the moisture to each strand.

- When blow-drying your hair, blast it with some cool air to help keep your hair cuticles smooth.

- Eat a diet rich in fruits, vegetables, and good fats, and take a daily multivitamin.

- Drink plenty of water. Just like your skin, your hair gets its moisture from your body. That means that if you want to keep your hair hydrated, you have to keep your body hydrated.

DAVE, my frizzy hair, my moist skin, and I went back to Bismarck, where we lived together as Mr. and Mrs. Nystul in my apartment. We were both eager to get on with our careers and move up that ladder.

Shortly afterward, Dave got a job in Minneapolis–St. Paul. The plan was for me to stay in Bismarck and look for a job in Minneapolis and then move once I found one, but I missed him too much, so I left my job in Bismarck and moved out a month later. Dave was working as an electronic news-gathering videographer at KSTP TV, and I got a job as an associate producer at *Good Company*, a daily talk show at the same station. It wasn't news, and I was no longer in front of the camera, but it was work, and really pretty enjoyable work at that. Working on a daily talk/variety show is never dull, given, well, the variety. Every guest and topic is different, so there's something new each day. The one fear I ever had about working was that each day would be the same, so *Good Company* was perfect.

About a year later, Dave and I talked about having a baby. It wasn't that my biological clock was ticking, but rather that I came from a big family and my parents already had fifteen grandchildren from my two older brothers and my older sister. I wanted my children to have cousins who were close in age. A part of me also wanted to "catch up" so that we and our children would be part of the big extended family. We tried, and then about a week later we reconsidered, agreeing that we probably should wait just a little while longer. We remembered those famous last words as we watched the lines change on the early pregnancy kit at home.

three

And Babies Make Six

I have to admit that when the pregnancy was confirmed by the doctor, I was slightly terrified. First of all, it was my first child. Second, I was determined to be a working mother. However, I had no role model to help blaze that trail. My mom, who had been a laboratory technician, stopped working when she had her first child. My sisters and sisters-in-law were all stay-at-home mothers, also. My intention made me question how I could be the pioneer with no family around as a support network.

Dave and I moved from our one-bedroom apartment in Minneapolis and bought a sweet little house in St. Paul, and although I loved the house, I still felt too far from my family. Even though our house was fully renovated (it was built in 1961), there were small repairs to be made. I was pregnant and Dave is not particularly handy. Over the years, this has become an endearing quality in him, because I have learned to live with it and because, as it turns out, I am the handy one. I've come to embrace that. But back then, I couldn't stand it. Both of our

Our first house, circa 1987

fathers were handy, so I guess he was just missing the gene. For example, we had a nice deck on the back of the house, but it had no railing.
It wasn't dangerously high off the ground, but high enough to take
a little spill if someone wandered close enough to the edge. Well, in addition to not being handy, Dave is also a procrastinator, and although I
asked him to please put up a railing, he still hadn't when I was nine-
plus months pregnant, lost my balance, and took a dive off the deck.
Luckily, it was early spring and there were still billows of snow on the
ground, so it was like falling into a giant pillow.

My favorite story about Dave's lack of proficiency in the repair arena
is the time he and our neighbor's husband set out to unearth a spigot
that was set down in a burrow in the yard. The neighborhood kids had
filled the hole with stones, making it impossible to access the spigot.
The two men were there for hours. They'd fashioned a "fishing pole"—
a stick covered with duct tape—and tried to fish out the rocks. Finally,
the neighbor's wife came out with a Shop-Vac, stuck the nozzle in the

hole, sucked up the rocks, packed up her Shop-Vac, and, without saying a word, went back inside.

WHAT TO DO IF YOUR HUSBAND ISN'T HANDY

There seems to be an assumption that all men are, or should be, handy. But they aren't. This is one of those situations in a marriage where expectations are everything. If there's one thing I've learned in twenty-seven years of marriage, it's that you have to manage your expectations. Just like you need to manage your time and your money. Managing expectations is about eliminating the gap between what we expect and what actually happens, and it will save you time, energy, anger, and frustration.

Try to see things from the other person's point of view. This doesn't mean that you must agree with each other all the time, but rather understand and respect each other's differences, points of view, and separate needs. So, that's my philosophical answer to "What to do if your husband isn't handy" . . . but since I'm all about practical solutions, here are some of those as well.

Find a Fix-It Man or Woman

Is anyone in the extended family handy? Maybe you can lean on them in a pinch and maybe a lesson or two will rub off on the unhandy hubby. Or maybe there's a handy friend or neighbor and you can do some bartering: Your unhandy husband can do some computer work for the computer-challenged neighbor handyman. It's also a good idea to ask friends and family for recommendations. As a last resort, check your local classifieds under *handyman*.

Do It Yourself

I'm not expecting anyone to know how to install their own water heater, but still, you should own a toolbox with the basics (hammer, screwdriver, wrench, pliers, power drill, assorted screws and nails) so that you can hang a picture, change out a doorknob, and put together a piece of "assembly required" furniture. Being able to fix things around the house without having to rely on *anyone* else (not just the hubster) is actually very empowering. When you want something done, it gets done. There are books out there that teach the basics. But stay away from gas and electricity. Leave that to the professionals.

I WORKED throughout my entire first pregnancy and felt really good except for a bit of morning sickness in the beginning. I didn't gain a lot of weight (a mere twelve pounds), so little that my doctor was a bit concerned and urged me to gain more. Erik was born ten days past my due date after thirty hours of labor and tipped the scale at a whopping nine pounds, thirteen ounces.

It was a Sunday morning, and his birth was announced on the evening news. The

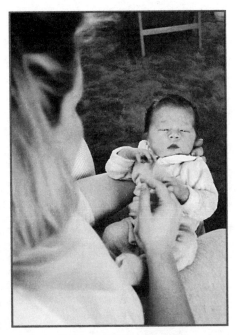

Baby Erik and me, 1989

station actually sent a crew to the hospital, and that night we tuned in to see ourselves on television with baby Erik and the newscaster announcing, "Our cameraman Dave Nystul and his wife, Jill, have a new addition to their family." My mother already had fifteen grandchildren and she was very excited that this was the first grandchild to make the news.

Mom had come to stay with us on my due date, never expecting that I would go ten days late, and three days after Erik was born, she went home. She just didn't feel right being away from my dad for so long. It was traumatic when she left. I drove her to the airport with the baby in the car seat and I cried all the way back home.

Years later, my mother said she blamed herself for leaving me so soon after Erik was born and felt that was the catalytic stressor for my later addiction. I've assured her that's not the reason, and it wasn't. Dave went back to work the day after Erik was born and had no choice but to work crazy shifts like three a.m. to noon, and so once my mom left, I was really alone. Dave would come home from work and just go to sleep, because if he didn't, he would get no sleep at all before having to get ready for work again at two in the morning. This meant that I was alone in the middle of the night *and* during the day while Dave slept. This routine was extremely tough on both of us. I was experiencing deep loneliness. And yet, despite feeling alone all the time, I also felt that even though I was literally and technically alone, there was still no "me time" where I could really concentrate on my own physical and emotional well-being.

FINDING TIME FOR YOU—
AND WHY IT MATTERS

Juggling home, kids, work, family, marriage, and volunteer work could be an Olympic sport. It is not for the faint of heart. But are we really doing ourselves, or our families, any favors by even attempting to "do it all"?

Whether we like it or not, Mom is the barometer for the general mood of the household. If Mom isn't having a good day, simply because she is such a central figure in the home, everyone else in the house is going to be affected by that in some way. It's a blessing and a curse. We can lift the entire mood of the house or drag it down without even really trying. I don't know about you, but when I am stressed and tired, I have a much shorter fuse and find dealing with the challenges of home and family that much harder. I don't want being a mother to feel like a burden, but it seems our instincts to be devoted moms often override the needs we have to take care of ourselves. In fact, as much as we need a break from time to time, our children need one, too. When we take time for ourselves, our kids learn to be more independent and appreciate what we do for them even more. We are also showing that taking care of ourselves is important.

You Are a Priority: Schedule "Me Time"

You are the first responder in your family. An emergency can come up at any time, and you should be as well rested and restored as you'd want your ER doc or EMT to be. Moms who take care of themselves before others are better able to take care of their loved ones, physically, mentally, emotionally, and spiritually.

Just like your standing hair appointment, pencil in downtime or "me time" as a perennially scheduled event. If you have to, drop one of the things in your jam-packed calendar to accommodate it. Your kids won't be scarred for life if they have one less home-cooked dinner during the week. Once you carve out this time, let your family know that, barring any emergency situation, you are not to be disturbed.

Rally the Troops!

Enlist the help of your spouse, your older kids, your parents, your babysitter—whoever is available—so that you can take a break. Trading babysitting with a neighbor or friend was a lifesaver for me when my kids were little and time and money were tight.

Grown-Up Story Time

I start to feel grumpy when I can't find time to read something other than a picture book for night-night. This is one thing that has helped me: Stash a book or magazine or the day's newspaper in the car (or keep one on your smartphone or Kindle) for those five- to ten-minute lulls in your day (for example, waiting at school pickup or for an appointment). It may not be hours of uninterrupted reading pleasure, but it's definitely better than none.

Call a Friend to Chat

This doesn't mean planning the bake sale or organizing the neighborhood watch—just talk, without an agenda. It's close to a real visit.

Plan a Long Walk with a Friend

Commit to it early in the week and honor the commitment. You're not training for anything, you're not trying to race-walk, you're just taking a long stroll with a good friend and enjoying the day.

I was in a constant state of anxiety to make sure that Erik's needs were properly met when he was an infant. To make matters worse, I missed my family back in California terribly. I had a few friends whom I'd met through our church, but no one who I could lean on. My work friends were mostly single, and the ones who were married were very career-oriented. In short, none of my friends had babies. That's a tough one for a new mother.

Having been raised in a family with four girls and only two boys, I never had the feeling of being outnumbered in the gender department. Who knew that eventually, in addition to my one husband, I would have three boys and only one girl? While this arrangement was all new at first, now, after twenty-five-plus years of raising three boys, I have gained a few insights into the process. For example, as rambunctious and physical as boys can be, they are all big teddy bears, especially when it comes to their mommy, which works for me!

SOME THINGS I HAVE LEARNED ABOUT RAISING BOYS

Show Affection

I listed this first because I think it's *so* important and something we tend to show less and less, especially as our boys get older and try to exert their independence. Find ways to show affection to your son, even if he acts like he doesn't want you to. Boys who grow up *getting* affection are more likely to *show* it later on in life. Not sure how to go about showing affection to your teenage (and older) boys? Hugs!

Kell, Sten, and Erik, 1999

Encourage Them to Show Emotion

Let your boys know that it's okay to cry and that home is a safe place to express emotions. Give your son unconditional love and support, and never shame him for expressing his feelings. Because society can pressure boys into repressing their emotions, knowing they can safely express their feelings at home is very important.

Let Them Play!

Boys tend to be more boisterous and active than girls. Play fighting and roughhousing are how they connect and express affection. Don't worry— it's normal, and Anthony T. DeBenedet, MD, in *The Art of Roughhousing*, says it's even healthy. This kind of physical interaction can foster positive relationships and promote intelligence—even if it means that stuff around the house is going to get broken. Also, expect to be visiting the emergency room a lot more than you ever expected to . . . but you will get used to it. Well, kind of.

Clothes and Shopping Are Much Easier and Cheaper

The array of adorable clothing available for dressing a little girl is virtually endless. It's fun, but it can be time-consuming and expensive. Dressing boys basically involves pants and shorts, T-shirts, and sneakers, with the occasional button-down or polo shirt thrown in for when they need to be dressed nicely. The savings, convenience, and lack of clothing "drama" cannot be overstated.

Less Drama and More Action!

Generally speaking, women and girls have complex emotional lives. Boys, on the other hand, tend to be mad, happy, or sad, and they run on only two speeds: fast and faster. Girls tend to function in all gears, including reverse. But don't expect to have long talks about the meaning of life with your boys until they're older . . . maybe.

Kell, Erik, and Sten, 2002

They Never Outgrow Superheroes

Boys, even at a young age, are captivated by superheroes. They sort out their identities in relation to the mythical characters they hear about. Even my twenty-five-year-old "boy" has a Thor bobblehead on his desk at work, and my thirty-four-year-old business partner and nephew always has been and always will be completely enamored with Superman.

Training to Be Gentlemen Begins with Mom

If we want our sons to be gentlemen, we have to be the ones to teach them how. Holding a door open, letting a lady go ahead of you, or giving up a seat for a lady are not things that come naturally. They must be taught. Resurrecting chivalry begins at home.

Having a first baby changes everything. Within moments, your world is altered dramatically and permanently, and there are no books on the planet that can *really* explain what you're going through. Suddenly, the driven career woman in me started to fade and the mother in me struggled to maintain equilibrium. I felt torn in a dozen different directions. I still had the same career dreams, but now I had new hopes and dreams that I'd never even considered before. I wanted to be the Perfect Mom, Perfect Wife, and Career Woman, but I had no idea how to do it all. It sounds silly, but the one practical chore that was truly overwhelming was the laundry: burp cloths, bumpers, sheets, towels, washcloths, my clothes, Dave's clothes, Erik's clothes . . . And every time Erik got the slightest bit of spit-up on him, I changed his outfit. The baby clothes had stains of every possible variety. I started to wonder if I would ever again wear a shirt where both shoulders didn't have some sort of yellowed stain. So much for my career-woman wardrobe. Then a friend gave me a great recipe for removing baby stains.

shirt soup

1 large stock pot (or a bucket)

Water

½ cup color-safe bleach powder (generic is fine)

½ cup dishwashing detergent (generic is fine)

1 cup vinegar

Fill the pot with water and heat (or use the bucket filled with hot water). Once the water reaches a boil, turn off the heat. Add the bleach powder and dishwashing detergent (slowly), and then the stained clothing. Let sit at least twenty-four hours. Check the stains; if they aren't

completely gone, dump out the water and repeat. Repeat the process until the stains are gone. This works 99 percent of the time.

When you are happy with the results, pour the contents of the pot (or bucket) into the washer and run through a regular cycle. Pour the vinegar into the fabric softener dispenser of your washer, or add it during the last rinse cycle. This will help prevent dirt and detergent residue from depositing onto clothing and causing more stains. If you can, dry the clothing on a clothesline in the sun. This will further lighten any stains and brighten your clothing.

I WAS AN ACE at stain removal, but not at breastfeeding. I tried to nurse Erik, but I just wasn't good at it. Even the Leche League woman who came to help me, at my mom's request, didn't help. I finally gave up on nursing when Erik was six weeks old, about two weeks after I had resumed work on the talk show. When I went back to work, my younger sister JoAnn came out to watch Erik. It was a stopgap measure. She had come to visit, and when I mused about what I would do with Erik when I returned to the show, we figured it out: JoAnn, who was working for my dad at the time, asked her "boss" to let her take a leave of absence. It was perfect, but I also knew that JoAnn, who was twenty-three, couldn't stay forever.

Although I was back at work and Erik was safely ensconced with my sister, I just didn't feel right. It was more than just the normal apprehension of being a new mother who is reluctant to go back to work. I didn't realize that I was suffering from postpartum anxiety. Honestly, my symptoms were so terrifying that I was reluctant to admit to anyone how devastating the feelings were. At first, I thought the anxiety had to do with my inability to nurse successfully—one of the reasons that I stopped after six weeks. And I felt guilty about stopping. Three parts of my personality that I own, for better or for worse: I am a worrywart; I often feel guilty, justifiably or not; and I am an overachiever. These qualities sometimes can manifest in positive ways, but in this case, it was particularly difficult for me to come to terms with being unable to nurse my own baby. It was a blow to my ego; I felt like a failure.

Switching over to a bottle did alleviate some of my anxiety, but just the anxiety that surrounded nursing. Clearly that was only one piece conquered. I tried to think logically: It is well-known that new moms suffer hormone shifts after giving birth, and certainly that could have been a reason for my anxiety. Still, that didn't comfort me, and what scared me, and was so disconcerting, was that neither my mother nor my older sister had ever suffered anything like this. I thought, *What is wrong with me?*

It really was a postpartum anxiety as opposed to depression. It wasn't that I couldn't get out of bed in the morning. As a matter of fact, being in bed made me more anxious. I needed to get out of the house and do things. I used to take Erik on long walks around Lake Como (Minnesota, not Italy, although the latter would have been lovely). We walked two or three miles several times a day. We took drives and went to shopping malls when the weather was inclement. I did anything I could to shake off the massive anxiety attacks that would cloak me in a feeling of impending doom. When Erik was about four months old, the feeling dissipated, but the thought of ever going through that sort of anxious panic again was nearly as terrifying.

When Erik was six months old, Dave and I moved to Huntington Beach. I felt mixed emotions. On one hand, that familiar feeling of homesickness had reached a fever pitch, so the move seemed a long time coming. On the other hand, the move seemed to be rather rash and precipitous given that Dave and I left two well-paying jobs in Minneapolis for freelance careers in California. JoAnn was around to help me in Minneapolis, but I couldn't depend on her forever; she had to go back to California and get on with her life. I felt as though I was skydiving without a parachute. I needed family and friends nearby. Dave agreed that being near family would be best for both of us and for Erik. We held a massive garage sale. As a matter of fact, I even sold my business/reporter wardrobe to a cross-dresser who happened by. We packed up a U-Haul truck and drove to California with six-month-old Erik in a car seat between us in the cab of the truck.

Erik was a seasoned traveler by then. We had already made a couple of trips. One time, we drove to see Dave's parents at their lake cottage in Detroit Lakes, Minnesota. It was a four-hour drive that took us about six hours because I felt it was necessary to take Erik out of his car seat every half hour to "stretch his legs." I also packed everything but the kitchen sink: baby swing, playpen, every article of clothing, formula, diapers, wipes, and even medications that we didn't need. Another time, when Erik was only about six weeks old, we flew to California. We got seats in one of those wide exit rows, and Erik lay at our feet on a blanket. In those days, airlines didn't require that an infant be in an actual seat at all (on a lap or otherwise). This time we also packed up all of Erik's belongings. You would have thought we were moving back to California then. We had *two* strollers, a Pack 'n Play, a baby monitor, and Erik's entire wardrobe. It was pretty crazy at the baggage claim. My mother had plenty of other grandchildren at that point, and even though I knew she had plenty of equipment at her house, I brought everything we owned . . . "just in case."

HOW TO KEEP YOUR SANITY WHEN
TRAVELING WITH SMALL CHILDREN

I recently attended a three-day conference that ended on a Saturday night, and I had to be up at four the following morning for a flight to Detroit. Needless to say, I took the opportunity to take a serious power nap on the flight and felt like a new woman afterward. But if I hadn't been prepared (earplugs, eye mask, blow-up neck pillow), I might have felt a little differently.

You see, there was a woman traveling with two small children (bless her heart!) who were *not* happy during most of the flight. My heart really went out to her. Although we didn't do a lot of traveling with our children when they were babies, we did enough to know it's stressful. My friend Reagan has traveled *extensively* with her two boys (now seven and five) ever since they were tiny babies. Here is some sage travel advice from the amazing Reagan—with love.

Have a bag/backpack for each child. Reagan calls it "the Arsenal," and it's filled with a DVD player, books, crayons, and a favorite toy. Headphones are good for the plane and car if the kids are watching a movie.

Add snacks to the Arsenal and carry some extras just in case. Bring whatever will make them happy at the time. Don't try to do the healthy thing when you're on a plane or long-distance road trip. Candy works just fine.

Bring an extra change of clothes and undies in a big ziplock bag. That way, if the clothes they are wearing get wet or pukey, you can zip them up and not have to smell them. Have a change of clothes for *each* child. Invariably, when one kid throws up, you know the next one will hurl right after.

Take the sick bags that are on the plane and put them in your car's glove box. Once, when my youngest got carsick just driving from our house to Salt Lake City because he didn't eat breakfast, I grabbed the bag just in time for him to use it.

Always **have wipes.** You'll use them about fifty times a day.

Depending on how old the kids are, talk about the expectations of the trip. Where you'll be going, fun activities you'll be doing, who will be there, how they need to behave. They get excited about all that lies ahead and will remember their manners more. When I find that my kids need reminding more than a couple of times, then I start to threaten and, if necessary, take away favorite toys. Such a bummer when you don't listen.

Deep breathing helps *you* **if your child is in a full-blown panic on the plane.** I also find that when I smile and apologize to people, they are more understanding. Once, when my two-year-old was a nightmare on the plane, I *almost* resorted to bribing the people seated around us with gifts. Now, at seven, he is the best traveler ever. They grow up so fast. The hard part is over before you know it.

Luckily, my parents' home in Huntington Harbor was large and able to accommodate us quite comfortably. There was a separate wing of the house that worked just perfectly for us. In fact, it was more like a huge apartment, with two bedrooms and a bathroom. Dave was freelancing and I was happily at home with him, Erik, JoAnn, and my parents. I felt a huge sense of relief and wondered if perhaps my postpartum anxiety had been a form of separation anxiety as well. With

Dave, Erik, newborn Britta, and me, 1991

the difficulties I experienced after having Baby #1 all but a distant memory, Dave and I decided we were ready to try for Baby #2. When I was pregnant with Erik, I went through prenatal classes with a woman who ended up having a girl named Britta. Ever since that time, I was secretly hoping for a little Britta of my own.

A little over a year later, I was pregnant. I was convinced that I wouldn't go through that dreadful postpartum anxiety again since I was at "home," but after my second child, a girl named Britta, was born, it hit me—out of the blue and with a fury.

What was *wrong* with me? There I was with my husband and beautiful children, living with my family, and stricken with paralyzing anxiety. I was thrown for a loop and so desperate that I went to my doctor for relief. He put me on Prozac, and it helped. The panic attacks were more short-lived and the anxiety steadily abated, but there were unpleasant side effects. For one, there was weight gain, and for another,

my libido was suppressed. More about all of this later, but both side effects were troublesome. Little did I know that was the beginning of a
vicious cycle where both weight gain and lack of libido fostered a different kind of angst. My self-esteem and my marriage suffered.

Now that we were a family of four, Dave and I rented a small house
a couple of miles from my parents' house. With two babies, my career
path was fading further and further into the distance. Having been
raised by a mother who was always at home, it was hard to imagine
doing it any other way. I think many women from my generation
struggled greatly with this. Many of us were raised by women who, in
the 1950s and 1960s, unquestionably stayed home.

My generation wanted something more, something different. Yet
we were conflicted. I found myself becoming resentful that my husband and I struggled financially because Dave's salary alone wasn't
sufficient. When we lived with my parents, they pretty much took care

My mother, 1970s

My mother and me, 1963

of us for meals, although we made contributions. Sometimes I went grocery shopping and added to whatever was in the house. We insisted on paying a monthly rent, even though they protested. But once we moved to the house in Huntington Beach after Britta was born, we were really on our own. I remember going to the supermarket with both kids in tow—one in the cart and one in the baby carrier—no longer having the luxury of leaving them with my mom. I had that same gray Honda Accord (she was thirteen when I finally gave her up), and now there were two infant seats in the back. It was a manual transmission and I had to shift and drive and pick up fallen pacifiers and bottles as I shifted. It was always a wild ride. And everything was so expensive, particularly diapers, formula, and baby food. I clipped coupons, checked prices, and made shopping lists for planned meals. We planted a small garden and canned tomatoes and used our own produce. My personality is such that if I see a problem or an obstacle in my path, I have to tackle it head-on and with a can-do, problem-solving attitude and sense of independence.

Family portrait, 1962

As the months went on, Dave's videography business began growing substantially, but I still wanted to contribute. Although I loved motherhood and my babies, I wanted more. This is where necessity is the mother of invention. I realized that there were not a lot of jobs that would pay me to work from home, but I was determined to make a go of it. I had to come up with a way to work from home where I could earn money and be my own boss. One of the main rea-

Our garden in Huntington Beach

sons I chose broadcast journalism as a career was the excitement and variety. The thought of working at a desk nine to five did not appeal to me. I wanted and needed to be my own boss. And I wanted to be with my babies as well.

The Internet was also a baby at that time. I decided to check it out. When the babies napped, I got online via CompuServe with our super-slow dial-up connection. I was immediately hooked to a whole new world. It was exactly the challenge I needed. I taught myself HTML coding and, using myself as a guinea pig, made a personal website. Then I took things further: If I could do this for myself, I could do this for others. And I could do it right in the comfort of my living room. I was on to something, for sure.

It all paid off in 1994 when Britta was around three. I wanted her to take ballet lessons, but we really couldn't afford them. I paid for a couple of classes for her at the local dance studio and then I pitched the idea to them of a website. It was the embryonic days of websites, and it was not yet on their radar. They were not only intrigued but gung ho. We bartered: I built and maintained their website and did a monthly online newsletter in exchange for Britta's classes. Pretty soon, I did the same thing for our gym, where I bartered for a membership. Pretty smooth of me. Working from home has many unexpected advantages. Who knows? You could even have a corner office with a view!

Britta as a ballerina, 1995

WAYS TO WORK FROM HOME

Tutoring

Were you one of those people who aced every math or science class? Consider tutoring.

Music Lessons

If you have the mastery of a musical instrument, consider giving music lessons in your home. Parents are very keen on giving their kids the traditional piano lesson as well as learning to play guitar, drums, clarinet . . . and let's not forget singing lessons. If you play, make it pay!

Arts and Crafts Classes

For both children and adults. You don't need any formal training or an extraordinary talent to teach people valuable skills and crafts such as lessons in couponing, computers, cooking, gardening, canning, knitting, crocheting, sewing, furniture refinishing, or anything else that intrigues you and your kids.

Web Design

Didn't go to school for this? Teach yourself with an online tutorial and then offer your design talents to local businesses for pay or barter. I might be a *tad* prejudiced in favor of this next idea, so forgive me ahead of time, but how about blogging? There's no limit as to what topics you have to choose from, but choose something that you love. It will make work more enjoyable and allow you to share your thoughts and ideas. And who knows where it will take you?

Graphic Design

You can teach yourself at home, although it does help if you have some artistic ability. I personally know *how* to do some graphic design, but my artistic sense is limited. I rely on those with more talent to do most of my graphics. Know where your strengths lie.

Scrapbooking

Are you a scrapbooker extraordinaire? Offering to help those of us who are *not* would be a great service.

Calligrapher

Perhaps you know (or can learn) calligraphy, or maybe you just have extraordinarily beautiful penmanship—consider addressing wedding and party invitations.

Photographer

This is possibly one of the best work-from-home options I am aware of (besides blogging). You set your own schedule, you don't need an office, and the equipment is minimal. I guess that's why there are so many talented mom photographers out there.

Kids' Party Planner

Plan kids' birthday parties for full-time working parents who don't have the time to do it themselves. Your children can go with you while you choose paper plates, party hats, and cupcakes.

Medical Billing

Medical billing courses can be taken at local colleges or online. Once certified, medical billers work in hospitals, physicians' offices, etc. Most certified medical billers work full time, though job hours are flexible. Some develop their own businesses so that they can work independently from home.

Bookkeeper

I don't know what I would do without my bookkeeper, Stacey, who is a work-at-home mom.

Furniture Builder/Restorer

I have a niece who has turned this into a work-at-home career. She finds old furniture with good "bones" and completely refinishes it and sells it. She loves doing it, she does it from home, and she turns a profit! Turn your garage or basement into a shop. You can hire some strong neighborhood kids to carry the furniture.

Gift Baskets

For the right person, this could be a great moneymaker. Especially if the baskets could be personalized for people's individual needs.

Artisanal Gifts

If you're a potter, painter, knitter, or dressmaker at heart, your skills can become a cottage industry for people looking for one-of-a-kind gifts. Baby blankets and sweaters, doll clothing, family portraits, or that perfect fruit bowl—everyone likes gifts and belongings that are one of a kind.

Social Media Manager

I hired my daughter, who recently graduated from college, to oversee all my social media. Her major was psychology, but she is a whiz at social media (as most kids are today) and does a fantastic job. If you love Twitter and Facebook, you could get paid for your social networking skills. Many companies and private citizens who blog are looking for social media–savvy individuals who can tweet and post Facebook messages to build their online audience. Keep an eye out for listings on sites like Mashable, or try contacting companies directly if their social media accounts seem a bit neglected.

WHEN ERIK was about to start kindergarten, we moved again. This time to Heber City, Utah. The California public schools weren't what they were when I was a kid, and everyone was sending their kids to private schools, which was simply unaffordable for us. We knew that

Britta and Erik, ages five and three

Erik holding baby Kell, 1995

the public schools in Utah were good ones. It so happened that my uncle was developing a subdivision in Heber City, and my sister Rebecca had already moved there about a year before. So, Dave and I packed up again, and while we waited for our house to be built, the four of us moved in with Rebecca and her husband and children. We were a total of four adults and seven children. Even with eleven people living under the same roof, I once again began to think about having another baby.

By this time, Britta was three and I felt like I was in a good place to add a final member (at the time, I planned on only three kids) to our brood. So it was there in Rebecca's basement that our third child was conceived.

I had stopped taking Prozac when Britta was about a year old, but with Baby #3, I was so terrified of a postpartum anxiety recurrence that I went back on it six weeks before I delivered. It helped a lot. Now, with one boy and one girl securely in the nest and my anxiety managed, I was delighted to be truly carefree about the new baby *and* its gender. We were thrilled to welcome the second Nystul boy, who generously arrived right after we moved into our new home and to whom we promptly assigned another Norwegian name, Kell.

Dave was establishing a new video production business in Utah, but still had his previous business in California, so he "commuted" and stayed with my brother Cole. The commute was a ten-hour drive, but flying wasn't an option because he needed to transport his equipment. Those were hard times. Dave was away *a lot*—sometimes he'd be gone for a week at a time or more and then come back only for a couple of days. Eventually, he got full-time work in Utah, but it was a tough road when I was alone with three little children. Even though Rebecca was close by, she was busy with her *five* children.

Sometimes I look back and wonder how I did it all by myself. I recall the general feeding frenzy at mealtimes and the challenge of getting Erik off to school with a good breakfast in the morning. To make matters worse, my kids were picky eaters and invariably someone didn't like the dinner I'd prepared. Breakfasts and lunches were less fraught, but dinner was tough. I remember crying out, "I'm not a short-order cook! The kitchen's closed!" But the truth is, the kitchen was never really closed. I should have been stricter, but if they didn't like their dinners, I confess that I made them something else. This was frustrating, not to mention tiring. So, what's a mother to do?

TAPAS FOR TOTS

My youngest is fifteen now, and I wish I'd thought of this before. The word *tapas* in Spanish means snacks or finger food. Since little kids don't eat a lot, tapas can be anything nutritious but bite-size. Rather than making one *big* dinner (especially if you have more than one child—odds are that everyone will not like the same thing), make a buffet of small plates. It's one way to please all the people all the time.

Mac and cheese in cupcake liners
Mini meatballs on a stick (toothpick)

Peanut butter and jelly or cream cheese and jelly rolled up like sushi or cut into shapes like trucks, hearts, flowers, etc., using a small cookie cutter

Grilled cheese cut into "soldiers"

Mini potato croquettes or pancakes

Homemade chicken fingers or nuggets (Panko crumbs are great for this.)

Creamed spinach mixed with cottage and American cheeses (They'll never know it's spinach.)

Fruit skewers with yogurt dip

Crispy fish "fingers" with creamy mayo dip

Frozen banana and/or grape chunks dipped in chocolate (or Nutella)

Watermelon cut into wedges shaped like pieces of pie—stick the
   rind edge into a stick and no one would ever know it wasn't a
   Popsicle
Veggie tortilla roll-ups
Mini pancake dunkers
Mini muffins placed on a stick and dipped into applesauce
Homemade breakfast bars

Since tapas are fun and tasty food, why not present them in a fun way,
too? Offer a nibble tray. Use an ice-cube tray, a muffin tin, or a compart-
mentalized dish and put tapas-size portions of food in each section.

Still stressed out about fussy eaters? *Relax.* Experts say that kids (especially toddlers) can become set on just about everything—including
the way food is prepared. If the peanut butter must be on top of the
jelly and you put the jelly on top of the peanut butter, be prepared for a
protest. Fortunately, this is a passing stage. Remember to breathe deeply
at mealtimes.

When Kell was just about to turn three, we went with my sister
Dori and her husband, Ken, to Disneyland. I confided to Dori that I
was "late" and puzzling over why. She laughed and said that I was
probably pregnant. I was in denial. "There is just no way," I insisted.
"That's impossible." I took the e.p.t, and sure enough, I was pregnant. I
was pretty devastated for about six months. Dave was thrilled.

My fourth child and third son, Sten, turned out to be my bonus
baby. He knows the whole story. He teases me that I didn't really want
him, but I always tell him that he was the best baby, and it's true. He
was such an angel. We often laugh because as the kids came along *one,
two, three, four,* we always took pictures and videos, but by the time we

Britta, Erik, and Kell with baby Sten, 1999

got down to Sten, the pictures and videos are fewer. One of my projects now is to organize all of the photographic memorabilia.

PRESERVING AND DISPLAYING DIGITAL MEMORIES

Advances in digital technology have made preserving memories an everyday occurrence. We can now capture anything in the moment directly onto our cell phones or digital cameras. The problem is that most of these pictures never go beyond that. Pictures are meant to be displayed, not locked up inside our computers, cameras, and mobile devices. Here are a few fun and interesting ways I've found for showing your favorite photos the light of day.

Scrapbook Without the Scraps

Even if you're not a supercrafty person, you can still make a supercool scrapbook using digital scrapbooking programs and websites. Digital scrapbooking takes less time and is less expensive than the paper alternative. Programs to consider are Mixbook and MemoryMixer.

Photo Books

Create one-of-a-kind photo books using your own family photos. There are dozens of online tools that let you group photos onto virtual pages, and then the book is auto-created within seconds. You can choose from different page layouts, backgrounds, and fonts, and also use photo tools to rotate, crop, adjust brightness/contrast, and other edits. Keep your "books" online, or order hardbound or softbound prints. Two good programs are Picaboo and Smilebox.

Digital Picture Frames

Printing out photos on your inkjet printer at home can leave a lot to be desired in the quality department. To display your prize photos in a higher resolution, consider a digital picture frame. They're essentially small storage and playback devices, but packed into a traditional-looking picture frame. Simply load up all of your favorite digital family memories, select a rate of playback, and put it on the end table for all to enjoy.

Instacreate with Your Instagram Photos

I rarely remember to bring my camera along on vacations, but I *always* have my iPhone, so I'm always snapping photos and sharing them on Instagram. The incredible popularity of Instagram has spawned endless apps and websites that help you bring your Instagrams from the virtual world into the real one. Here are a few of my favorites:

- **InstaShirt.me:** Make custom tees from your Instagram photos.
- **Sticky9:** Convert your Instagrams into a pack of nine magnets.

- **ImageSnap:** Convert your Instagrams into 2 x 2-inch ceramic tiles.
- **ArtFlakes:** Convert your Instagrams into 4 x 4-inch vinyl stickers that are fully removable.

You can also have your Instagram photos printed and display them in a number of different ways:

- Good old-fashioned wall displays.
- Make a photo clothesline: Cut a section of wire or string to span the space you want to cover. Attach the two ends of the wire or string to the wall with thumbtacks or hooks, pulling it taut, then hang your photos with some clips. This is like a clothesline for photographs, and you can change the "laundry" at any time.
- Use binder (butterfly) clips to make photo stands for your desk.
- Don't like to clutter your walls with photos? Stick photos on the inside doors of closets and kitchen cupboards.

- Use a flower frog to display individual photos. Flower frogs are usually made of wire and sit at the bottom of a bowl or a vase to hold flower arrangements firmly in place. They make a great photo arranger, too.
- Turn your favorite photo into a life-size photo decal for your wall.
- Use multiple images as wallpaper for an accent wall.
- Rather than displaying a bunch of photos, why not blow up one favorite photo as the backdrop for a room?
- Give new life to 4 x 6 prints by displaying them on a framed corkboard.
- The easiest way to make a photo display look neat is to make a photo grid on the wall using identical frames.
- Clipboards are always a unique choice for photo displays.
- Take your favorite photos and blow them up onto canvas at your local copy center. Instant art!

Finally, I feel compelled to say a word about *storing* your digital photos. As I have sadly had to learn the hard way, photo files can be easily erased with the push of a button or a computer hard drive crash. Thanks to "cloud" storage you can protect your most precious memories. Cloud storage is basically just storing something online, but in a safer way that isn't so easily crashed or lost. There are also free cloud storage services such as Photobucket and Snapfish. But still, don't forget to print out your favorites every few months.

I hope something here has inspired you to start thinking about ways to give your photos—and memories—the attention they deserve. If nothing else, get them off of your computer, print a whole bunch of 4 x 6 prints, and fill a beautiful box with them for your coffee table.

. . .

HERE COMES the hard part in what was the stay-at-home-mom dream story. About nine months before my fourth pregnancy, when Kell was two and a half, he started soaking through his diapers and clothing. I got bigger and thicker diapers, and still, he soaked right through them. I couldn't understand what was going on. One afternoon, Rebecca and I went with our kids to a McDonald's PlayPlace. Kell sat on my lap while the other kids played. He was nearly listless. In the several days before, I'd noticed that his tummy was distended and his arms looked scrawny, but when he didn't want to play that afternoon, my instinct told me that something was wrong. I immediately called my doctor to explain Kell's symptoms and asked Rebecca to watch the other kids. As Kell and I drove to the doctor, my mind ran wild. I thought of every horrible childhood disease.

The first order of business at the doctor's office was a finger stick. Kell's blood sugar was over 600. Normal is 80 to 100. The doctor knew what it was immediately. He was somber as he said, "I am so sorry; Kell has diabetes." I have to admit that, at the time, I didn't understand the enormity of the disease—especially for such a young child. To me, it wasn't the kind of life-threatening disease I had feared and imagined while driving to the doctor's office. I was actually relieved that this was something that could be managed. That feeling was short-lived, since the next thing the doctor did was send us to the hospital.

four

Diagnosis Diabetes

Our pediatrician wanted to call an ambulance to take Kell and me to Primary Children's Hospital in Salt Lake City, but I preferred to drive Kell there myself. The truth is, we had no medical insurance at that point in our lives, and I knew that an ambulance would cost thousands of dollars. Rebecca had been watching my kids while Kell and I were with the doctor, so I drove to her house, picked her up, and left her older kids to watch my younger ones. Rebecca drove to the hospital while I sat in the back with Kell. He was strapped in his car seat, an intravenous line in his skinny little arm, the IV bag draped over the garment rack hook. I was realistic enough to know that I could not make this trip alone given that not only was I an emotional wreck, but what if Kell had a crisis as he sat in the backseat and I was busy driving on the highway?

I wished Dave was there and I kept thinking that it never seemed to fail that Dave was out of town whenever there was any kind of a crisis, and this was a crisis bigger than any other I had experienced. But Dave was in an RV en route to the *Late Show with David Letterman* in

New York City to shoot a special segment. A part of me understood that it was impossible for him to just jump ship and come home. Another part of me thought that I would have just abandoned the project to come home for my spouse and child. I was resentful, something that Dave and I have since explored in therapy. At the time, I felt abandoned and alone. My logical mind knew that Dave had no choice but to be away, but it was hard to accept. Little did I know that there the seeds were planted for our personal difficulty that lay ahead.

It was a seemingly endless drive to the hospital. To this day, I can't remember whether we entered through the main entrance or the emergency room. I just remember that we were directed to a wonderful endocrinologist named Dr. Lindsay, a sweet and tender older man with a big full beard. By the time we appeared before Dr. Lindsay I was beside myself, but Dr. Lindsay's manner soothed me immediately. He assured me that although diabetes can be life-threatening in the worst-case scenario, if we took good care and control—control being the most essential ingredient—Kell would be fine. I appreciated his words deeply.

Kell was admitted to the hospital under Dr. Lindsay's care. We stayed for the next five days as Kell was stabilized and I was educated about the care of a diabetic child and the disease in general. I slept in a chair in Kell's room, but really, I barely slept. I was frightened, and my head was spinning to the point that when I commandeered Rebecca for the drive, I'd neglected to even grab Kell's bottle, which he still took comfort in, even at thirty months old. At the time, I had no idea that we would be admitted to the hospital, but still, I didn't even think of bringing a bottle for the drive. Needless to say, Kell was weaned off the bottle pretty fast, since the hospital apparently didn't think he needed one at his age and I was too overwhelmed to think to ask. He was such a little trouper. There was never a cry or a peep out of him, even without the bottle and as he was constantly getting needles in his arm and pricks in his fingertips.

Kell at the hospital with another patient, 1998

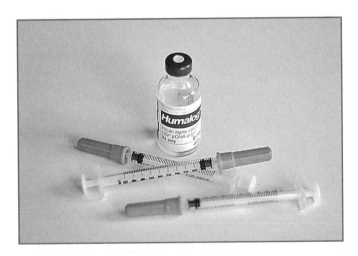

Kell's shots and insulin

The Certified Diabetes Educators (CDE) on staff at the hospital taught me how to give an insulin shot. At first, I practiced on an orange. Easy to give a shot to an orange. When the time came for me to administer the shot to Kell, I was way outside my comfort zone. The shots were injected into either the fatty part of his thigh or arm, but Kell was such a scrawny little thing that there really wasn't ample fat and I felt like I was hurting him. If Kell hadn't been as cooperative as he was, I don't know that I would have done so well. Because of Kell and the fact that I am nothing if not persistent, I became an expert in no time at all. I also came to realize that with each shot, I was doing the opposite of hurting my child—I was saving him.

Kell looked better by the time he and I left the hospital. He was no longer listless; his belly looked normal; his urine output was normal. But I was afraid to leave the hospital. I was afraid to make the drive. I was just plain afraid to handle this, and my fear was exponential in Dave's absence. (He was still on the Letterman project, which included a cross-country RV trip with the crew. It was the last job in the world that allowed crew members to hop on a plane home on a dime.)

I stopped at a convenience store before we got on the highway and bought peanut butter crackers and a bunch of juice boxes. I was so worried that his blood sugar would go low and I needed reinforcements. Juice boxes were my lifeline for years. He was in the backseat in his car seat facing forward, and I was talking to him all the time and probably looking more in the rearview than I did ahead on the way home.

With this experience, my role changed instantly: I was now not only a wife and the mother of three, but also a full-time, 24/7 nurse. The hospital had given me reams of paperwork with instructions and dietary recommendations. In my crash course, I developed an understanding of the disease. I also had a modicum of guilt. Irrationally, and despite the medical evidence, I felt that I had done something wrong with Kell. In most cases there is a genetic link, and I wasn't convinced of my innocence until I found out that Dave's grandmother had type 1 diabetes back in the day when medicine wasn't what it is now. His poor grandmother ended up having a leg amputated. Part of me thought, *Aha! It's Dave's fault.* I laugh now. But poor Dave . . . he couldn't win with me back then.

The genetic link was powerful, but there was also a bona fide trigger for the onset of the disease that might otherwise have remained dormant for a while: Kell had recently had ear tubes put in his ears. That sort of trauma, although mild, can impact the hypothalamus and the endocrine system of a child who is genetically predisposed to diabetes.

I went from knowing nothing at all about diabetes to knowing more than I wished I would ever *have* to know. The most compelling information in my personal armory was distinguishing between fact and fiction. One thing is for certain: Regardless of the kind of procedure your child may have, never be shy about asking questions or stating a preexisting condition that your child may have, as innocuous as it may seem.

COMMON MISCONCEPTIONS ABOUT KIDS WITH DIABETES

Type 1 and type 2 diabetes are often thought of as the same, but they are two *very* different diseases. There are many myths and misconceptions about type 1 that can be very frustrating to the children who have it and their parents. Here are a few of the most annoying ones:

Eating Too Much Sugar Causes Diabetes

Type 1 diabetes is believed to be caused by a mix of genetic, immune, and possibly environmental factors. Although researchers have identified some patterns, the root cause of type 1 diabetes is still unclear. But we know for certain it is not caused by an excess intake of sugar. Having an immediate family member with type 1 diabetes also increases the risk of diabetes.

Type 1 and 2 Are the Same—the Only Difference Is the Age Group

You cannot compare type 1 diabetes to type 2, because they are not the same. Children with type 1 diabetes are completely insulin-dependent because their bodies have completely destroyed all their insulin-producing cells, while those with type 2 still produce insulin—either not enough or the body no longer absorbs it properly. They may have to take insulin, but can usually also control their condition with other combinations of medications, diet, and exercise.

Diet and Exercise Can Cure Diabetes

Currently, type 1 diabetes is incurable. There is no way to reverse it, naturally or otherwise (at least for now). Any website or book claiming it's possible is wrong.

People with Type 1 Diabetes Can't Eat Sugar

People with type 1 diabetes take insulin and they can eat sugar. However, most type 2 diabetics do not take insulin and need to regulate their sugar intake. Type 1 diabetics can eat virtually any food they want as long as they are mindful of portion sizes and give themselves enough insulin to cover it. The more carbohydrates eaten, the more blood glucose will rise. Some foods raise blood sugar faster than others, according to the glycemic index. A healthy meal plan for people with diabetes is the same for those without diabetes: vegetables, fruits, whole grains, and lean meats with modest amounts of salt and sugar.

Taking Insulin Cures Diabetes

People with type 1 diabetes take insulin because their pancreas no longer makes enough insulin to keep their body functioning properly. Without their daily injections they would not be able to live. So insulin is a needed medicine, but it is not a cure. There is progress toward finding a cure, but to date there is no cure for diabetes.

Only Children Get Type 1 Diabetes

The majority of type 1 diabetics are children and adolescents, but anyone can develop type 1 diabetes at any age.

Nights were no longer the same—a phase that lasted for a long time. Although I was accustomed to being awakened by infants and small children, nights with Kell were an entirely different story. I'd set my alarm for two-thirty a.m. so that I could creep into his room and stick his finger to get a glucose level. Fortunately, Kell slept right through. He was such a sound sleeper and had become so accustomed to this ritual that he could literally respond without breaking full consciousness. I would go in to check if he was low, hold a juice box to his lips while he unconsciously sipped, and then I'd retest him with another prick a half hour later. Through it all, he didn't make a peep.

There were a few times when Kell had convulsions because his sugar was low and I didn't catch it in time despite the regimen of our schedule. But still, I never had to call 911. I knew what to do. The amazing thing was that my instincts—both maternal and learned—were so finely honed that I always went to check him just as he was convulsing, preempting the two-thirty a.m. check-in. Something deep inside me would wake before the alarm and send me to check on him early. When he convulsed, I would sprint for the fridge in sheer panic, grab a juice pack, and literally pour juice down Kell's throat. To say it was terrifying would be an understatement. I was physically and emotionally exhausted.

CARING FOR KIDS WITH CHRONIC ILLNESSES (WITHOUT LOSING YOUR MIND)

Parenting *healthy* children is challenging and sometimes overwhelming, but parenting a child with a chronic illness takes *overwhelming* and *difficult* to new and amplified levels. Some examples of chronic illnesses include diabetes, asthma, cerebral palsy, cystic fibrosis, and cancer. While these conditions are all very different, the children and families affected by them have a lot in common. The whole family must come to terms with the illness and manage to keep it all together despite frequent changes in schedules and priorities. The stress of caring for a child with a chronic illness is considerable. Hopefully, these tips will help ease the strain a little bit and help you, your child, and your whole family to cope.

Become an Expert!

One of the very first things I did after learning about Kell's type 1 diabetes diagnosis was start researching. I read everything I could get my hands (or eyes) on. If my child was going to have to deal with this disease, I was going to learn all there was to know about how to care for him. The more information parents and children have, the less frightening the present and future will seem. Knowledge is empowering. It can help both you and your youngster feel more in control of the condition you are both facing.

Seek Out Support Groups

I can't stress the importance of this enough. Sometimes what helps most is simply knowing that you're not alone. There are many websites and organizations available to help provide you with information and support and lead you to others who can empathize and provide support. Right after Kell was diagnosed, I found www.childrenwithdiabetes.com, an online support group, and it made all the difference. Suddenly, I had a worldwide network of parents that I could go to with questions, or just to talk, any time, day or night. Through that network, I made lifelong friends. I also learned about new studies and technology and connected with hopeful and inspiring circumstances that I wouldn't have by simply going to quarterly doctor appointments with our endocrinologist. This truly was a salvation for Kell and our family.

Communicate

There is no better way to ease fears and to build trust with your child than to communicate openly and honestly about their illness and any medical procedures they may have to go through. Keep the information you share age-appropriate, and don't forget to inform the rest of the family. The chronic illness of a family member affects everyone. Keeping open lines of communication with your family can help ease fears and stress.

Keep Your Child Involved with Friends

Illness often interferes with routines and activities, and friendships are often casualties. Keeping kids involved with their peers and making an extra effort to maintain friendships can go a long way in helping them cope. Friendships help children to feel normal and provide identities separate from their illnesses. Seek out opportunities for your child to connect with other kids with the same or similar illnesses. Most major hospitals and clinics can help you find support groups. ChildrenWith Diabetes.com holds annual conferences called Friends for Life, designed specifically so that children with the shared common denominator of diabetes can get together and compare notes and just have fun. These kids truly do become friends for life.

Coordinate with Your Child's School

Good communication with your child's school is essential when you have a child with special health needs. There are many things you and your school can do to help prepare. Each year before school started, I would call the school and set up a time to meet with Kell's teacher and the school district nurse and lunch aides. I would give them some very basic training, a printed cheat sheet of signs to look for indicating high or low blood sugar, and all of our emergency contact information. I tried not to overwhelm them with volumes of information, but provided just enough to make them feel more comfortable and to keep Kell safe.

Remember Your Other Children

Parents need to be mindful of the need to give time and attention to other children in the family and still meet the needs of their chronically ill sibling. Your other children may experience jealousy, anger, and even depression. It's important that you address their concerns and make sure they don't feel pushed aside.

Encourage Independence

Some families inadvertently foster dependency because they find it easier to provide the care for their child, rather than teaching him to care for himself. Don't deprive your child of the important and rewarding experience of learning to care for himself. Instill pride and self-confidence that will prepare children for adult life.

Remember to Also Take Care of Yourself

Parents who are caregivers need to take good care of themselves—otherwise, they won't be able to give good care. Just as you are flexible and understanding with your child, be the same way with yourself. When things are getting too hard to handle, sometimes it helps to take a time-out. Give yourself time to do something you enjoy. Exercise is a good way to clear your mind and release tension.

Let Others Help

Many friends and family members are looking for opportunities to help. Take advantage of these. They take some of the stress off you while strengthening your relationships. Turn to them when you are in need of support and strength. You might also want to take advantage of respite care, a short-term specialized child care that allows parents to take a break from their sometimes overwhelming responsibilities.

ALTHOUGH I NEVER gained significant weight during my pregnancies, I gained weight after each baby. After Kell was born, I was determined to reverse the process and lost about fifty pounds. I was feeling pretty good about myself . . . and then I was pregnant again. About a year after Sten was born and on the heels of Kell's diagnosis, my weight was out of control. It was a combo of sleep deprivation and nightly snacking on chips and sour cream–based dips. I needed to take control and I needed something to improve my mood. At this time in my life, salty, crunchy snacks were my substance of choice.

I did my research and drove to a clinic in Salt Lake City, where I was evaluated and accepted as a candidate for bariatric surgery. I knew that I was done having babies, and I felt that bariatric surgery was the thing I needed to stop me from gaining any more weight and also to develop a lifestyle rather than depending on diets. Luckily for me, my surgery was performed laparoscopically, and so my recovery was relatively easy. After the surgery, not only did I not want to eat as much as before, but if I did, I didn't feel well. Subsequently, I lost one hundred pounds. I am five-feet-ten, and I went from a size 20 to a size 12. At one point, I was a size 8, yet I quickly realized that was an unrealistic weight for me to maintain.

At my new size 12, I was happy with my body. I was going to the gym almost every day. My sister dubbed me the "stair step queen." It was the perfect machine for me, because it didn't put pressure on my

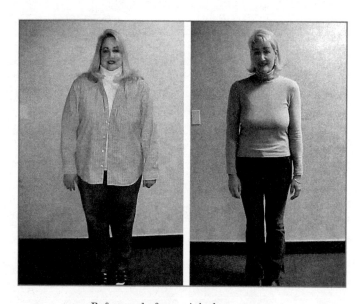

Before and after weight-loss surgery

bad foot. Most people don't like the StairMaster, but for me, there is something about climbing that makes me feel in control.

Those days on the StairMaster provided me with motivation, but I was also fatigued a lot. When I was really dragging, I would occasionally resort to energy drinks to pull me through. The problem was that they always made me feel sick after I drank them. So, I started researching natural lifestyle alternatives to energy drinks and was pleasantly surprised at all the options out there, the majority of which I would never have imagined. The next time you need a boost, try a natural energy booster instead of drinks full of sugar, caffeine, and chemicals.

SURPRISING ALL-NATURAL ENERGY BOOSTERS!

Pump Up the Volume

I find that listening to music for about an hour a day helps to reduce fatigue. Your mental and physical energy get a big boost every time you immerse yourself in music that moves you.

Color Your World

Yellow is the color most closely linked with a healthy mood; other happy hues are orange and lilac. Try painting your walls in these colors or, if you don't want to paint an entire room, accent a wall or paint just your ceiling blue. Blue simulates the sky and brings the outside in.

According to research published in the *Journal of Orthomolecular Psychiatry*, the colors you *wear* also affect how you feel. Tap in to red to help you exude confidence. Seek out orange for its playful, high-energy qualities. If you like wearing all black, accent your outfit with colors. Instant pick-me-up!

Take a Whiff

The scent of jasmine increases beta waves, which make you more awake and alert. Keep a small bottle of jasmine essential oil in your handbag. Or try a whiff of peppermint. A study in the *Journal of the International Society of Sports Nutrition* found that sniffing peppermint essential oil immediately improves both athletes' running speed and office workers' typing speed. Its scent boosts motivation and concentration. So grab an infusion of peppermint, whether it's a breath mint, lip gloss, or hand lotion. Orange, lemon, and cinnamon are also energy-boosting scents. Aromatherapy scents can easily be ordered online or found in many health food or homeopathic stores.

Take a Bite out of Life

Cool and tangy citrus flavors can ramp up your energy by activating nerves in the mouth, throat, and nasal cavity that trigger a heightened level of brain activity. Chewing gum is another way to enhance energy. The muscle tension that comes with chewing can increase heart rate and alertness and stimulate the nervous system.

Tap Your Thymus

Your thymus gland is located at the top center of your chest, below the collarbone, between your breasts. Tapping on this gland results in production of T cells that boost energy and relieve stress. To get an instant boost of energy, it is recommended to tap your thymus with the fingertips for at least twenty seconds. Plus, while you tap, make sure that you are breathing slowly and deeply.

In the Blink of an Eye

The next time you're fighting the urge to doze off at your desk, try blinking more often. When reading, watching TV, or on the computer, blink ten to twenty times per minute, rather than staring at the screen or page without blinking at all. (You'd be surprised how little we blink when staring at our screens.)

Inhale . . . Exhale

Take a few deep breaths when you feel your energy level dropping. Stop what you are doing and pay attention to your breath moving in and out of your body. By taking time to pause instead of rushing, hurrying, and worrying, you give yourself a chance to rest and recharge.

Exercise with a Buddy . . . Outdoors

Studies show that the energizing effect of exercise is boosted when done with a partner. Ditto when exercise occurs outdoors.

Turn Your World Upside Down

Even if you're just leaning over to touch your toes, any inverted pose is energizing. It stretches out your back and increases the blood flow to your head.

End Your Shower with a Burst of Cold Water

Your body responds more quickly to a cold stimulus than to hot, so a quick, short blast will perk you up.

Pull Your Hair

No, really . . . *Gently* take handfuls of hair and pull the skin away from your scalp to get blood flowing to that area of the head. This can relieve a lot of tension that can be very tiring.

Be Nice to a Stranger

When we behave kindly to others, our energy goes up. Find lots of ideas for joining the acts of kindness movement at www.randomactsof kindness.org.

Have a Good Laugh

After a good laugh, you experience a momentary surge of energy, which—in addition to reducing stress and boosting immunity—can help your body regenerate more healthful cells over time. A hearty belly laugh increases your heart rate and activates your muscular system, making you feel instantly revived. It also provides a shift in thought patterns, and since energy levels are directly related to the way people think, it can be very uplifting. So go ahead, yuk it up!

Flower Power

Buy blooms or grow them in your own garden. A study at Harvard Medical School showed that flowers not only make a room look prettier but also lift the mood of everyone around. It also showed that people who looked at fresh blooms in the morning reported higher energy levels for the rest of the day.

Remember to Eat

Research has shown that people who eat breakfast have more energy and are happier throughout the day. Furthermore, if you eat every three hours instead of just a few times per day, you are more likely to see your energy levels sustain themselves.

Drink Less Alcohol and More Water

Even only slight dehydration can cause feelings of extreme fatigue. Drinking water steadily throughout the day can do wonders for energy levels. Also, drinking alcohol close to bedtime will lead you to feel especially fatigued the next day. Alcohol interferes with the ability to sleep deeply, even if it helps the initial falling-asleep process.

Eliminate Energy Vampires

Ever get off the phone with someone and instantly want to hit the sack? Then you've been bitten by an energy vampire, someone who drains your lifeblood. Avoid them.

Let the Sun Shine In

Studies show that a mere twenty minutes a day of sunshine can work wonders to boost your energy—and your mood. You can also get an energy kick from sitting near a light box for forty-five minutes a day. It's a pill-free way to increase alertness during waking hours.

Tidy Up Your Work Space

Clutter can sap the energy right out of you. Start by clearing everything off your desk and dusting and cleaning the surface. Now pick and choose carefully what you put back and where you put it. Keeping items to a minimum will boost your attention for the items that remain there.

Think Positive Thoughts

Scientists have proven that we have around sixty thousand thoughts a day, and the vast majority of those are negative, which rob us of precious energy. Try consciously replacing "I can't" thoughts with "I can" thoughts. Practice it over and over for one week. You'll be amazed at how much more energy you have.

Change It Up

Drive a different route to work, get a new hairstyle, and try a different workout. Not only will you feel more energized, but as studies show, changing your routine makes you smarter, too.

Reflexology

Take a golf ball and roll it between your desktop and your hand, from the base of the thumb, where your hand webs out, down to the wrist. There's a really sensitive spot there. Stimulating it will perk you up.

Sit Up Straight

Poor posture puts uneven pressure on the spine and causes some muscles to work extra hard, which makes them tight and tense and requires them to use up extra energy. You can realign your spine by simply lifting your rib cage away from the top of your hips.

Make Sure You're Getting Enough Iron

Due to certain conditions such as anemia, women often feel fatigued. Getting more iron helps fight that condition. Ideally, you'll get what you need from iron-rich food sources like kale and spinach, as well as whole grains, beans, red meat, fish, and tofu. But if you're like me and require iron supplements, talk to your doctor first.

There you have it—a whole list of all-natural energy boosters to keep you going when your energy tank is empty.

BARIATRIC SURGERY relieved stress in terms of my self-image, but the biggest stress relief happened when Kell was seven and got the insulin pump. That was when our lives really changed for the better. The insulin pump, a catheter placed under the skin, works a bit like a pancreas in that it releases small amounts of insulin 24/7. The doses are divided into basal rates, bolus doses to cover carbohydrates in meals, and correctional and supplemental doses. It keeps blood glucose levels in range with far more control than shots alone could ever do. Some people warned that the pump would be more work, but I found it easier, and Kell caught on quickly. We were simply required to program doses of insulin into the pump based on the food that Kell was eating. He knew to give himself a bolus dose of insulin to cover the carbs in his meals.

We saw Kell's endocrinologist every three months to determine the efficacy and reset the pump as Kell grew and his dietary intake changed. Ultimately, it was wonderful, but in the beginning and until I was assured that Kell was a pro, I wasn't able to rely on the pump's automatic integrity with complete confidence. I went to Kell's school every day at lunchtime to administer the bolus. It was stressful to run back and forth with baby Sten in tow. And then I had a brainstorm: I took a job outside my professional realm in customer service at the UPS Store for the simple reason that the UPS Store was right next to the school. The extra income was also a welcome boon.

I left Sten with my friend Ashley, who ran a day care out of her house. Sten was the first child I ever put in day care, so that was a little traumatic for me, and guilt-producing. I worried that I was putting Kell's illness in front of my younger, healthy child, but at the end of the day, I knew that this solution was best for everyone. Sten was in a familiar place and happy; I was gainfully employed and close to the school. I was right there—just in case.

The problem was that after a day of work and a day of childcare, plus a night of cooking and laundry and helping with homework, I was beyond tired. I recently ran across an article about making your own bath bombs that involved using essential oils (like eucalyptus) and dropping them in the tub to help sick kids feel better. I admit, when I saw the recipe, the first thing that came to my mind was, *Okay, but what about mommy?* All you moms know what I'm talking about. When your kids are sick, you're tense. If mom feels better, kids feel better. I loved the idea of making my own bath products, and made a slight change to the recipe: Instead of adding eucalyptus essential oil, I substituted lavender. Lavender is known for its ability to help calm stress and anxiety and to help promote sleep. Most day spas are scented with lavender. So these bombs are for you, Mom. It's not quite as good as the Caribbean, but it's like a mini vacation in the tub.

homemade bath bombs for stressed moms

Vitamin E oil, an antioxidant, preserves the oils in this recipe. Borax, a naturally occurring mineral powder, which you can find in the laundry aisle of your supermarket, acts as an emulsifier to bind the oil and water. Liquid witch hazel, distilled from the witch hazel plant, is a natural astringent with skin-healing properties, and in this recipe acts as a binder for the dry ingredients. It doesn't come in a spray bottle; you will have to put it in one. For the molds, I used some fun silicone ones in the shape of hearts and flowers that I ordered from Amazon, but you could really use any kind of mold, even a small (¼ cup) measuring cup.

1 cup baking soda

½ cup cornstarch

½ cup citric acid

¾ tbsp water

2½ tbsp sunflower or other light oil, such as almond oil

20 to 30 drops of lavender essential oil

¼ tsp vitamin E oil (optional, but recommended)

¼ tsp borax

Vegetable or other natural colorant (optional, if you don't feel like messing with color)

Witch hazel in a spray bottle

Molds

Mix the baking soda and cornstarch together until completely combined and smooth. (I grind up oats in my blender and add about ¼ cup of those, too. They give the bombs a cool textured look and are good for your skin as well.)

Whisk the citric acid, water, oils, colorant, and borax together in a large bowl.

Drizzle the wet ingredients slowly onto the dry ingredients and blend thoroughly. Mix with your hands until all of the ingredients are combined.

Lightly spray the mixture two or three times with witch hazel. The mixture should just start to hold together when pressed in your hand, like slightly moist fine sand. If it's not sticking together, spray a little more witch hazel.

Pack tightly into molds. Let the bath bombs dry and harden overnight before you pick them up. I got a little impatient (who, me?) and tried to take them out of the molds only a few hours later, and they would not cooperate. In the morning, however, the ones I had left alone were hard as rocks. Silly me. No worries, though; the crumbly stuff works just as well in the bath. This recipe made about sixteen bath bombs, each 1⅝ inches in diameter.

. . .

LIFE IS ALWAYS a series of adjustments, and as I became more comfortable with the pump, I allowed myself to rely not only on that device but on other people as well. The school nurse, Kell's teachers, and the lunchroom aides were a tremendous support system. I felt confident that they could handle Kell's condition. My children were now roughly four, eight, twelve, and fourteen, and the appeal of what had once been my dream to be a working mother materialized again. I began to send out résumés. I needed to work again within my field.

The whole family, 2002

My friend Ruthie, who was also my roommate at BYU, was a local anchor for Channel 4 (KTVX) and passed along my résumé to the executive producer of a talk show called *Good Things Utah*. Shortly after that, the show's producer, George Severson, called me. He had grown

up watching *Good Company*, the show that I'd produced in Minnesota.
I was hired.

With a toddler, a diabetic child, one prepubescent girl, and one
full-fledged teenager, I went back to work with a bag filled with mixed
feelings—excited to get back into my career, but conflicted with the
sense that I was jumping ship. Logistically, I knew it could work. Dave
was teaching at BYU in Provo, which was luckily only a half-hour
drive from home. My studio was a one-hour drive away. I would have
to leave the house at five in the morning, and Dave could get the kids
off to school. I could then be home around two-thirty, in time to pick
them up. Not to mention that we could use the extra income, and with
my newfound faith in Kell's support group at school, this seemed like a
great idea. I dove right in, ignoring the obvious fact that I wasn't super-
woman. My body was yearning for rest, but I figured I could forge
ahead despite the sleep deprivation.

Not only did my return to the workforce give me a whole new outlook on life, so did turning forty . . . and they happened at the same
time. I daresay there isn't a person on the face of the earth who doesn't
feel the impact of four-oh. For me, I was living the dream of the working mother. I felt confident in myself for the first time in years. But I
was now forty, and it was a good time to take stock. As I studied the
inventory of my life with greater conviction, one of the casualties was
less tolerance for aspects of my marriage that I'd previously accepted.

Although Dave and I historically struggled financially and my salary was helpful, I resented that Dave didn't make enough to support us
on his own. Sure, I wanted to work, but I wanted my earnings to be
mine. I felt that I had paid my dues as a full-time wife and mother.
Looking back, I realize that I was being irrational and even a little ridiculous. I see now that my resentment stemmed from the fact that

Dave and I were *both* working full time, but I was still doing all the domestic chores: laundry, grocery shopping, cooking, helping the kids with homework, and still being the primary—if not sole—caregiver for Kell. When it came to Kell's diabetes, Dave had just checked out. I felt overburdened and resentful. Counseling later helped us with this, and Dave is a different person now. He is *so* helpful, and that has made a huge difference to me. But at the time, we argued incessantly, although we were careful not to argue in front of the kids. Really, we were *both* terrible communicators. When I was angry, I gave Dave the silent treatment, which isn't helpful at all.

I didn't shirk my responsibilities at home, but my life outside the house changed. There was a rebellion that welled up inside me, and I was not the same person. There was my restored career as a working mother, a clearly failing marriage, a remaining lack of libido from the Prozac, dealing with my child's diabetes, financial struggles, turning forty, and that prophetic first glass of wine as I socialized in my "new" life with my work friends. I wish I'd had a crystal ball. I didn't see all the contributing factors that led me right into the eye of a perfect storm.

five

Thanksgiving

By this time, I had ignored all the negative aspects of my life and the proverbial writing on the wall. Kell and I were dealing well with his diabetes, and it was under control. My weight was under control as well, and I looked and felt good about myself. (Or at least I thought I did.) I loved working on the television show. I met fascinating people from all walks of life who were guests on *Good Things Utah*, like the cast of the Harry Potter movies, Dr. Laura, and Jane Seymour, to name a few. I'd even won a regional Emmy Award for Best Feature Program. I had a new group of friends among my coworkers and started hanging out with them in the evenings as we toasted fellow workers who were leaving or being promoted. Until then, celebrations in my life had been dry. Going out and drinking socially was not only a departure from my small-town life in Heber City but also a deviation from my upbringing—an era in my life that I now characterize as simply "before."

In retrospect, I suppose that my new lifestyle was a form of delayed teen rebellion. I was always the almost perfect child who stayed within

Sten, Kell, and me with my Emmy, 2001

the social boundaries of my LDS world. I did well enough scholastically
to attend a fine LDS university, married a good and decent man (with
whom I was head over heels in love), and had four beautiful children.
But suddenly, I had a desire for something more. When I first moved
to North Dakota and joined the work force, I went out with some colleagues a few times and would have a couple of drinks. But I quickly
decided it wasn't for me. Now, the decision to go out and drink socially
came more naturally. It was easy to go out and party with my coworkers. It was a decision that was neither conscious nor unconscious: Everyone was drinking, and I was merely fitting in. I was a grown-up, and as
such, I felt that I was allowed to seize certain freedoms regardless of
the doctrine of both my church and my family. It was as though there
were two of me, and one was justifying my freedom while the other
was sabotaging my belief system.

What I learned from bitter personal experience is that there is no
faster way to unhappiness than to act against your beliefs. When we

betray our beliefs it creates inner conflict, and we feel divided instead of whole. Our ability to believe is part of being human. You cannot choose to believe or not to believe, but you can choose *what* to believe. Discovering (or rediscovering) yourself and your beliefs isn't something you accomplish in a day. It's likely a matter of trial and error.

Here are a few tips for how to start that process. And keep in mind that it is a process. Trust me, I've been through it.

DISCOVERING (OR REDISCOVERING) YOUR BELIEF SYSTEM

Remove bad habits from your life. Some examples: drinking to excess, drugs, smoking, overeating, overspending. Those bad habits create an illusion of escape.

Accept that you cannot please everyone. As long as you continue to live your life to fulfill other people's ideas of who you should be, you'll never be the true you. I love this quote by Raymond Hull: "He who trims himself to suit everyone will soon whittle himself away."

Start trusting your own judgment and decision-making abilities. Sure, you're going to make mistakes, but it's through mistakes that you learn and grow.

Be alone with you. In our ever-increasingly technology-driven world, it is becoming more and more difficult to unplug. All the noise makes it impossible to really contemplate your life. Take some time each day just to think and reflect. Whether you take a walk, sit on a park bench, or meditate, remove yourself from the distractions of life and give yourself time to just be alone.

Spend some time writing about your life—past, present, or future. My mother has always been an advocate of keeping a journal. Writing in a journal or diary forces you to crystallize your thoughts into words on paper, and that forces you to think deeper about your life experiences. Keep a notebook that's easy to access and update. It will be a source by which you can measure your growth throughout your life, and it will be a precious record for your children.

Start *doing* the things you believe in. Don't just think about them; take action. This will confirm what you truly believe in.

Serve others. Mahatma Gandhi once said that "the best way to find yourself is to lose yourself in the service of others." I can personally attest to this. The day I entered the Ark, the staff and residents were busy wrapping and sorting gifts to give to the needy for Christmas. It could not have been a better way to ease my entry into voluntary "incarceration." As I helped wrap boxes and choose age-appropriate presents for kids who wouldn't otherwise have any presents, I began to forget about all my problems and began to think about how much I had to be grateful for. Service to other people and to the community is the ultimate way to find purpose in your life.

Ralph Waldo Emerson famously said that "life is a journey, not a destination." Finding yourself is a journey, not a destination. There will be stops and starts along the way, but it is *my* belief that living what you believe is the path to your ultimate happiness.

Notice that I say *my* belief. Once I strayed from my core belief system, the one that was steeped in me from childhood, I became lost. I was looking for something else that was bigger and better. But, like Dorothy in Oz,

I realized that there was no place like home, and home for me was there all along in my heart, although in a slightly different form. Things looked different and I saw things with a greater and changed perspective, and that made all the difference for me, but my original belief system remained intact.

In addition to my nights out with coworkers, I began to travel on my own. Friends for Life, our diabetes support group, holds conventions at different locations around the country, and Kell and I would often go to connect with other diabetic kids and their parents, many of whom I had already become friends with. I'd always loved to travel. During the heyday of my father's business, my family traveled a lot. I remember one weekend when we flew off in my dad's private jet to San Francisco, where we celebrated my little sister's eighth birthday. There were other trips as well, to England, Spain, Morocco, and France. By the time high school came around, I was so bitten by the travel bug that I seriously considered becoming a travel agent. The ability to travel significantly waned once I left home and certainly when I got married and had children, the latter of which squashed any sense of abandon. Not to mention that Dave and I couldn't possibly afford lavish family vacations.

So here I was, jetting off to this place and that place and having alcohol-fueled parties with coworkers; my marriage gradually suffered the fallout. Alcohol is subtly seductive. It can be most cunning to anyone unwittingly susceptible to its addictive aspects, as I was. I recall one trip in particular, to Key West, drinking margaritas at sunset. Under the influence, it was easy to forget about the kids who were at home with their father while their paternal grandfather lay dying in Fargo. It was easy to ignore the fact that Dave had to leave the kids home alone when he flew off to be with his father and console his mother. I was snorkeling, shopping, eating, and partying. The more I drank, the more I rationalized that my behavior was justified and acceptable and the more I was able to forget the sad reality, which is that I was deeply unhappy.

I know sometimes it can feel like our happiness is at the mercy of outside influences over which we have no control, but there are actually some *very simple* things we can do to make our lives not only happier but more purposeful, fulfilling, and even simply sufficient.

TEN THINGS WE CAN DO TO MAKE LIFE HAPPY, PURPOSEFUL, AND FULFILLING

Be Grateful . . . and Keep a Journal of It

Start with just one line a day in a gratitude journal. Include the smallest details (putting on comfy clothes after a long day of work) or the biggest blessings (your health, your family). Just a few seconds a day is all it takes, and research has found that people who get into the habit of writing down good things that have happened to them every week show a significant rise in happiness.

Be Social . . . and I'm *Not* Talking *Media*

Call at least one friend or family member a day. Texts and e-mails do not count! Make an actual phone call to a loved one, just to chat and catch up. We humans are social beings, and studies show that socializing with our loved ones makes us feel better. Having close bonds with other people is one of the most important keys to happiness.

Start the Day with Intention

Henry Ford said, "Whether you think you can, or you think you can't—you're right." Well, that same philosophy holds true for living a happy life. Life is dictated by your expectations. If your first thought when you wake up in the morning is "Today's going to be a great day!" guess what? You're probably going to have a great day. The opposite holds true as well when it comes to negativity. So use that. Before you get up each morning, set an intention for the day. It could be anything—even something as simple as "Today I will savor the little things" or "Today I will say thank you to important people in my life." In *The Art of Happiness*, the Dalai Lama says, "Every day, think as you wake up: Today I am fortunate to be alive, I have a precious human life, I am not going to waste it."

Stop Comparing Yourself

While keeping up with the Joneses is part of American culture, comparing ourselves with others can be damaging to happiness and self-esteem. Instead of comparing ourselves to others, focusing on our own personal achievements leads to greater satisfaction.

Give People the Benefit of the Doubt

If we give people the benefit of the doubt and believe they have our best interests at heart, we may occasionally be wrong, but for the most part we feel appreciative and peaceful. On the other hand, if we assume the worst of people, we walk around feeling suspicious and critical. I'll take the former, thank you.

Do a Good Deed

It's a well-known fact: When you do good, you feel good. Simple gestures such as helping a neighbor, volunteering, or donating goods and services result in a "helper's high." You get more health benefits than you would from exercising or quitting smoking. In addition, people who volunteer for selfless reasons live longer and have stronger relationships.

Exercise Your Right to Be Happy

A Duke University study shows that exercise may be just as effective as drugs in treating depression (with no negative side effects). Other research shows that in addition to health benefits, regular exercise offers a sense of accomplishment and opportunity for social interaction, releases feel-good endorphins, and boosts self-esteem.

Take a Walk Down Memory Lane

Savoring happy memories is one of the secrets of the happiest people. Remembering happy times simply makes us happy again. This is why we love photo albums and sharing our pictures online and why so much of our memory-making time with friends and family is spent reminiscing. Feeling a little down? Let your mind drift down memory lane. It works!

Get Silly!

Text your significant other with a silly picture of yourself. Post "What made you smile today?" on your Facebook page. Wear brightly colored socks. If your pants are long, wear a different color on each foot. Use the search functionality on Twitter and look for *happy* or *smile*. Laugh out loud. Seriously, just choose to laugh and keep going. People-watch and make up conversations in your head about what they might be thinking.

Text a friend, "What's the funniest thing you've heard today?" Blast your favorite music and dance around with absolutely no regard for rhythm or appearance. (Thanks to tinybuddha.com for a lot of these ideas.)

Take Time to Connect

Whatever your spiritual beliefs, studies show that connecting to a Higher Power correlates with happiness. Just stepping back to realize that we are part of an enormous universe can put some perspective back into life. Spend a few minutes each day contemplating something larger than yourself. Take a walk in nature. Cultivate a sense of being blessed and feeling grateful.

Don't Overthink Happiness

Hyperfocusing on happiness can, ironically, make people less happy. A study found that women who focused exclusively on being happy had trouble actually achieving it. Possible reasons given were that they set their happiness standards too high or they focused on personal happiness at the expense of things that truly make people happy, like relationships with friends and family. So, just a reminder to focus on the happiness, rather than the pursuit thereof.

(Okay, that was eleven, I know.)

Dave knew that I was drinking socially, and as my social drinking got heavier, my marriage got rockier, and Dave was both disapproving and frightened. He made a literal leap of faith when he converted to LDS because it meant so much to me and my family, but now he embraced what had become his own faith so deeply. Drinking not only disregarded every tenet of our family's value system but defied our LDS faith. Church had been a pivotal part of my life since childhood, and I stopped going. Dave and I argued bitterly and incessantly. Although we tried to hide our arguments from our children, kids can hear you, and certainly sense the turmoil, even behind closed doors. My drinking was causing an enormous rift between us: Dave insisted that drinking wasn't what "we did," and I felt that he was being extremely judgmental.

My life wasn't turning out as planned. The things that I once wanted were not what I wanted anymore. My arguments with Dave were escalating, and one night, an argument grew into an ugly fight. I don't swear. I don't use curse words. But that night, I used the *F* word directed at Dave as he confronted me about my drinking. The more that Dave chastised me, the more I dug in my heels. I told Dave that I wanted out of our marriage. I wanted a divorce.

After that fight, I stormed out of the house, went to a restaurant in town, alone, and got drunk. That was the first time that it was difficult to deny that I had a drinking problem. I was desperate and sad and life as I knew it was crumbling, if not crashing down, around me. I knew where the town AA meeting was held, as I had looked it up previously while contemplating the idea. This time I somehow made my way over to the building. When I got there, however, I couldn't make myself walk in the door. Admittedly, I was drunk, but I was more than impaired. I felt helpless as the alcohol all but paralyzed me with fear, preventing me from entering the room. I sat down on the floor in the hallway, not knowing what to do.

Suddenly, the door opened and an older gentleman named Roland stepped out into the hallway. He looked at me as if he'd expected to find me there, and then he simply reached out his hand, pulled me up, and silently took me inside to the meeting. In retrospect, I realize that wasn't AA protocol, but he must have had an instinct about me. We've since become friends and agree that it was clearly intuition that told him there was another lost soul in need of comfort and support. I went to only one more AA meeting during that phase. I needed way more help than AA could give me.

After my solo night at the bar, and despite AA and Roland's intervention, my life was suddenly fraught with turmoil and falling apart. Dave's and my spiritual separation became a physical one, and he moved to an apartment nearby. I had also quit my job at the talk show after five years, giving myself the simple reason that it was becoming too stressful to be that far away from the children and home. Plus, the hour-long commute was fine in the summers, but the winter drives could be brutal if there was a snowstorm. There were also the couple of times when Kell had diabetic crises while at school and driving there was harrowing. Looking back, I had a ton of excuses for quitting, except for the real one: my drinking. I never admitted that the drive was also too long to make it home drunk. Denial is a beautiful thing, and coupled with alcohol, it is an even stronger cocktail.

But I needed to work. We needed the income, and I needed some semblance of stability. I took a job as community coordinator for a national telephone directory publisher that was only about two miles from our home. It was a real departure from the pulse of broadcast journalism. There was still room for creativity with a little design work here and there, but the level of creativity simply wasn't the same. So, in that two-mile drive, I made my first stop at a liquor store. Until then, my drinking was relegated to the occasional restaurant where I sat solo at a bar, evenings out with coworkers, or at conventions with Friends for Life. Now, I felt the desperation of *needing* a drink. More than just one. I didn't want to be at home without alcohol. It wasn't just about my job. It wasn't just about Kell's diabetes. It wasn't just about any one thing. It was a confluence of events and emotions that led me—for the first time that I can remember—to drink with the intention of going numb.

The store was about halfway between work and home, and I bought myself a box of white wine. The box was a deliberate choice: The kids would be home, and I felt that a box would be easier to seal and hide than a bottle. I slipped into my room, shut the door, and poured myself a drink. As the alcohol flowed through my system, I felt the pain subside. I thought if one drink made the pain abate, another would be even more satisfying. I didn't finish the entire box this time, but I drank enough to feel sufficiently numb. When I cooked dinner that night for the kids, I was drunk.

And thus the cycle: Depressed and anxious, an addict goes for the bottle; depressed and anxious because of the hangover, the addict goes for the bottle again.

As someone who has experienced her fair share of anxiety both sober and drunk, I'm here to tell you that it's not fun. Your heart pounds, you hyperventilate, and your mind tells you that something terrible is about to occur. Anxiety can hit you like a bolt out of the blue and can be quite debilitating. But that doesn't mean you need to be heading to the medicine or liquor cabinets for relief. There are many safe nondrug remedies for anxiety that are effective. Here are some of my newly discovered favorites.

NATURAL REMEDIES FOR ANXIETY

Chamomile

A cup of chamomile tea can help to calm the nerves. Some compounds in chamomile bind to the same brain receptors as drugs like Valium.

Valerian

Valerian is a sleep aid that contains sedative compounds. If you want to try it, take it in the evening—not before you go to work. Valerian is often combined with other sedative herbs, such as hops, chamomile, and lemon balm. It can be purchased anywhere you buy vitamins and supplements, but always check in with your physician before taking any herbs or supplements.

Lemon Balm

Lemon balm has been used since medieval times to reduce stress and anxiety and help with sleep. Lemon balm essential oil can be purchased

at any natural foods or health foods store. The best way to apply essential oil is on the bottoms of your feet, or you can diffuse it into the air with a diffuser.

Oxygen

If you are experiencing anxiety, it is nearly impossible to breathe—almost by definition. However, if you can learn to identify anxiety as it comes on, there are breathing exercises that can help you to focus and intentionally calm down.

Try this: Exhale completely through your mouth, and then inhale through your nose for a count of four. Hold your breath for a count of seven. Now let it out slowly through your mouth for a count of eight. Repeat at least twice a day. Get into the habit of doing this even when you aren't experiencing overwhelming anxiety. If you do frequently experience anxiety attacks, try carrying a paper bag in your pocket or handbag. Blowing in and out of a paper bag forces you to take long, slow breaths from the diaphragm, creating a calming effect.

Hungry? Check In with Your Appetite

Many people experience anxiety when their blood sugar is out of whack. This can happen if we have eaten too much of the wrong kinds of foods or if we've simply neglected to nourish ourselves (or nourish ourselves properly) throughout the day. Take a moment to check in with what you have—or have not—eaten that day and perhaps grab a healthy snack that will balance your blood sugar. Omega-3s are a wonderful solution. Researchers at Ohio State University discovered that taking 2.5 grams of omega-3s (or having twelve to fifteen ounces of salmon) can reduce stress and anxiety by more than 20 percent. That's good enough for me.

Stop Stinkin' Thinkin'!

When anxiety attacks, the most important thing you can do is stop and realize where you are, what you are doing, and why this is happening while you take a few deep breaths. Remind yourself that your terror is just the anxiety talking and not reality.

Heat Things Up!

Think about how relaxed you feel after spending time in a sauna or steam room or lying on a beach in the midday sun. Heating up your body reduces muscle tension and anxiety. A warm bath can help relax the muscles, ease aches and pains, and give you quiet time to think—all that heat just melts away anxiety.

Talk It Out

Talking about your anxiety with a mental health professional, a clergy-person, or even just a close friend can go a long way when it comes to relief. If this doesn't help, or the anxiety worsens after "talk therapy," there might be a more serious underlying medical cause. In that case, take the conversation to your physician. And remember, while anxiety can be discouraging, it doesn't need to be debilitating.

Wait It Out

When an impulse you need to control is strong, waiting it out is usually enough to keep yourself in control. As a rule, if you wait at least ten minutes before succumbing to temptation, you'll often find that strong impulse is now barely a thought.

The Olfactory

The power of scent is a remarkable thing. It invokes such strong feelings that once you associate a particular smell with a certain emotion (think of the feeling of warmth and security associated with Mom's freshly baked cookies), simply smelling it in the future can evoke those same emotions. The power of scent can benefit our health as well. Our sense of smell can actually connect to the brain and affect our mood and sense of well-being.

Aromatherapy utilizes essential oils, also known as plant hormones. The inhaled aroma from these oils stimulates the limbic system in the brain. The limbic system is a region that influences emotions and memories and is directly linked to the adrenals, pituitary gland, and the hypothalamus—the parts of the body that regulate heart rate, blood pressure, stress, memory, hormone balance, and breathing. This is the reason that the effects of essential oils are so immediate in bringing about emotional and physiological balance.

The array of essential oils that are available is almost mind-boggling, and each has its own healing properties, such as antibacterial, antiviral, diuretic, vasodilator, tranquilizing, and adrenal-stimulating. Luckily people much smarter than I am have figured out what oils produce what effect.

The following three aromatherapy recipes are good examples of how different oils can actually affect our moods. Plus, they sound like they could come in handy when life gets a little out of balance. It all makes perfect "scents."

make your own aromatherapy mood mists

You'll need mini spray bottles and distilled water to prepare these.

QUICK ENERGY BOOSTER
1 drop eucalyptus essential oil
2 drops lemon essential oil

2 drops geranium essential oil

3 drops peppermint essential oil

Total Tranquillity

2 drops bergamot essential oil

1 drop jasmine essential oil

3 drops lavender essential oil

3 drops geranium essential oil

Antianxiety

2 drops each of: lavender, jasmine, geranium, ylang-ylang, and
  bergamot

To make the mists: Fill a mini spray bottle with 4 ounces of pure distilled water.

Carefully put the selected blend of essential oils directly into the spray bottle.

Shake vigorously to combine.

Be sure to shake the bottle before each use, as the water and essential oils tend to separate. Use in a diffuser, add to a hot bath, or massage onto the bottoms of your feet.

AFTER DAVE MOVED OUT, my drinking intensified. On my worst days, I consumed an entire box of wine, drinking surreptitiously in my bedroom behind a closed door or in the garage (one of my favorite hiding places for my wine). As time wore on, I became more brazen and poured the wine into a red plastic cup, thinking that no one would know what liquid was in there. I figured that the kids would think it was my usual Diet Coke. But the kids smelled the wine on me despite my minted breath from toothpaste and mouthwash. For sure, the two oldest children were aware of what was happening. Erik was furious and called me out. Britta was more protective and tried to make excuses for me. It was clear to all of my children that my behavior was altered. Going into my room and shutting the door? Shutting out my children wasn't me. When Dave had the kids on the weekends, although it's nearly unfathomable now, I drank even more to mask the loneliness.

My life has changed since those days, although each day is an exercise in conscious effort. Understand that I certainly don't make light of the difficulty people like me go through as they combat addictions. But it's the little things now that help me to make life *smoother.*

HOW TO MAKE A GREAT SMOOTHIE

In my opinion, smoothies are the perfect food. They are perfect for a quick breakfast or a healthy snack and absolutely delicious. When I first started making smoothies, I simply threw a banana, a carton of yogurt, a splash of orange juice, and some ice into the blender. That still works, but I've found there are healthier and even more delicious ways to make a smoothie. Keep in mind, however, that even though smoothies are often a healthy alternative, it is still important to be mindful of what is in them. Some of the smoothies they offer in stores—even "healthy" stores— can be loaded with fat and calories. Be smart, and if you go for the indulgence, perhaps you can do so as a snack or dessert and cut back on the portion size.

Choose fruits that are naturally sweet, like pineapple, berries, peaches, and mangos. Cut them up and freeze them and you won't have to add ice cubes that will water down the smoothie. Skip the agave, honey,

and raw sugar because these are all still just sugar.

To beef up your smoothie with protein, just add Greek yogurt (go for low-fat or nonfat). Greek yogurt is my *favorite* kind of yogurt. It's creamy and delicious and it has three times as much protein as regular yogurt.

Instead of fruit juice, add in a splash of coconut water or almond milk to your smoothie. It's the perfect substitute for calorie-laden juices. Coconut water is rich in potassium and electrolytes, and almond milk, which comes in a variety of flavors, adds sweetness,

plus it's a good source of calcium
that's low in calories and free of
saturated fat.

Bananas are the go-to fruit for
most smoothie lovers, but most
bananas are actually equal to two
servings of fruit, so it is easy to
overdo it. To switch things up, try
a quarter of an avocado instead.
Avocado will make your smoothie
extra smooth and is loaded with
nutrients, including potassium,
B-complex vitamins, antioxidants,
and fiber. While avocados are high

in fat, it's healthy fat, which in moderation helps lower LDL cholesterol
and raise healthy HDL cholesterol.

Finally, add a pinch of cinnamon to spice up your smoothie. Cinnamon not only lends sweetness but also has antimicrobial properties,
helps with digestion, and can help control blood sugar levels.

These tips are a good place to start, but as you get more comfortable
at smoothie-making, try new fruits, flavors, and combinations to find
your own perfect recipe.

BONUS TIP: To ensure all your wonderful ingredients are the perfect
consistency and texture, blend them until the liquid is *fully circulating*
within the blender for at least five to ten seconds. The liquid at the top
should be swirling and diffusing back down to the bottom. It can take up
to forty-five seconds for this to happen, depending on the power of your
motor and how full the jar is. Make sure you don't have too much in
your jar (it shouldn't be more than two-thirds full) or your blender will

never achieve proper circulation, even with the most powerful motor. Happy blending!

It's all admittedly hazy as I look back. It was a time when my thinking was not at all smooth (forgive the pun). My life was spiraling out of control. I even got a DUI and lost my license for ninety days. I barely recall the circumstances except that it was my parents who rescued me. (Isn't it always?) They were in their seventies at the time, and as (my) luck would have it, they had moved from California to Provo. After the drunk-driving incident, they would pick me up every morning and drive me to work—and then come back every afternoon to take me home. Neither the DUI nor my parents' kindness was a deterrent. I kept drinking. I was the definition of an addict.

Despite my drinking and my battles with Dave and our differences, neither one of us ever really wanted the separation. We had been apart for nearly a year when a bouquet of flowers arrived at my office one afternoon. A big, beautiful spring bouquet sprinkled with my favorite— gerbera daisies. It was from Dave, with a card that said I was the one who came first in his life. Not the kids and not the church, but me. Many of our arguments centered on my feeling that I wasn't a priority for Dave. On this day, my defenses were already down: I knew that I missed him and missed who we were as a couple and who we all were as a family, but after I read the card, I remembered just how much. To this day, this memory makes me cry.

I didn't call him right away. Rather, I tried to digest it all. The next day was Friday, and when Dave came to pick up the kids for the weekend, I walked up to the window of his car. I thanked him for the flowers and the card and we small-talked a bit. When he dropped off the kids on Sunday, we went for a drive and talked for hours. We didn't address what tore us apart, but we talked like we had in the old days—about nothing and everything.

Over the next month, we started seeing each other, but we didn't tell the kids. We wanted to be sure that we were "meant to be" once again. We didn't want to give the kids any false hopes until we were certain we could make it work. That was like dating him all over again. Like a second honeymoon. I would go to his apartment, and for sure, those clandestine times alone reignited our love. But I still had one stipulation: I needed him to understand and accept me for who I was, because I still wasn't ready to give up drinking or go back to church. Maybe Dave figured that he'd effect a change in me or maybe he didn't realize the extent of my addiction, because he agreed.

About a month after our first "date," we sat the kids down in the family room and told them that we would be a family again. The boys were thrilled and happy, although they played it a little cool, not wanting to be too emotional. Britta got mad, though. She said, "After what you put us through and we're finally adjusting and now you're getting back together?" But of course, she was happy. Dave moved back in, and I not only kept drinking but also stepped up my game. In fact, I was drinking so much that I could no longer *remotely* deny to myself that something was terribly wrong. I was out of control.

Despite my previous DUI, there were still times when I was on the road and should not have been. Every morning, I told myself, "Today I won't drink," and every day, I failed. At night, I passed out. Sure, I passed out in my own bed, but that's still passing out. In the mornings, I was always hungover and horribly anxious, and the only remedy was to have another drink. Dave was beside himself, increasingly unable to stick to our agreement to accept me no matter what. My drinking was no longer a secret: Rebecca lectured me. My brother Kevin insisted that

I speak with a counselor or therapist. He never mentioned my drinking specifically; he just said that talking to a professional might be "good for me" and gave me a phone number. I called and made an appointment for one day after work. On the way, I stopped for some drinks, and when I got back on the road, I was too impaired to follow the directions to the counselor's office. My brother and my parents called me later to ask if I had gone. I explained that I didn't because I'd gotten lost. My father, always my champion and mentor, called me a drunk. I hung up on him. And then I got in my car, thinking to myself, *You want to see a drunk? I'll show you a drunk!* and proceeded to drive to Park City, where I bought two boxes of wine. I was so angry at everyone. I didn't want to go home. I shut off my cell phone and pulled into the parking lot of a Holiday Inn Express and drank wine until I could barely see straight. That was the night before Thanksgiving. We were all due to celebrate at my parents' house in Provo the next day.

On Thanksgiving morning, I woke up on a couch in the lobby of the Holiday Inn with someone's coat wrapped around me. I had no recollection of how I'd gotten there. I was horrified. I rose from the couch and handed the coat to the desk clerk, asking him to please give it to whomever it belonged. I went to my car, planning to drive home to Heber City, but I simply could not bring myself to go home. Instead, I drank the remainder of the wine as I drove the back roads in circles. I pushed away the thought that it was Thanksgiving and I was supposed to be celebrating with my family.

I got home that Thanksgiving night around seven. Honestly, it's all a drunken blur. I just remember that it was dark outside. I don't know how I even made it home in one piece. When I walked into my house, everyone was waiting for me. They were relieved to see me. I had been missing for twenty-four hours with my cell phone deliberately and defiantly turned off. My family didn't know whether I was dead or alive. Later, their relief turned to justifiable anger. I simply retreated to my room to pass out.

The next morning when I woke up, the house was empty. I made my way to the kitchen, expecting to find a note of explanation as to where everyone had gone. Instead, there was a boldly printed note on the kitchen counter with the name *Jeremy* and a phone number. Somehow, I knew the name and number were meant for me. Shaking, I picked up the phone and dialed. Jeremy answered with his name, and I said who I was. Jeremy explained that he was the admissions officer at a rehab center called the Ark and asked what he could do for me. I said, "I have a problem and need some help." Jeremy asked if I would come to see him the next day. I didn't know at the time that Dave was the one who found the Ark for me. He stumbled upon this particular place somewhat serendipitously, in fact. He had been looking into our insurance coverage, knowing I needed some sort of medical intervention, and the person assisting him had a wife who overcame her addiction at the Ark.

On Saturday morning, Dave drove me to the Ark, where we met with Jeremy. That was the first day of the rest of my new life.

six

The Ark

The Ark was about an hour's drive from home. It was a beautiful winter morning when Dave and I drove there for my appointment with Jeremy. As Dave drove, I just looked at the hilly panoramic vista; there wasn't too much conversation.

The Ark

The Ark itself was tough to find, nestled in a residential area replete with winding roads. When we finally arrived, there was a gate with a call box. Dave pressed the button, announced our arrival, and the gate swung open. Despite the bucolic setting, I had a moment of terror as I realized that if an electronic gate let you in, then it also had to let you out. At the top of the driveway sat the Ark, a sprawling five-thousand-square-foot home with painted white wood siding and blue trim set amid snow-covered gardens that I would later discover are magnificent when in full bloom.

Jeremy greeted us. He was in his middle thirties, with an athletic build, dark hair, and a warm smile. Once in his office, Dave and I sat on the couch and Jeremy sat behind his desk in a chair. He wanted my story. I was open and honest. I told him not only about the recent event of Thanksgiving Day, but also about the dark road I'd traveled for years. I assumed he would advise counseling sessions and outpatient treatment, but after hearing my story, Jeremy suggested that I become an inpatient for thirty days.

That's when I became unglued. I literally fell back on the couch and wept. That was the last thing I wanted to hear. The notion of what I felt was incarceration scared me to death. How could I leave my kids? How could anyone function without me? What about my job? I'd lose my job. It was just overwhelming. When I got my wits about me, I asked (nearly pleading) if I could do outpatient treatment. Jeremy responded with a kind but firm no. Had I staunchly refused to do inpatient treatment, I'm pretty sure that Jeremy would have agreed to outpatient as better than nothing, but he and I both knew what I needed, and despite my pleading, his insistence prevailed. There was no doubt in his mind that I required far more intense intervention. I tried to bargain the time down to three weeks as I did the math and realized that thirty days would run into Christmas. How could I be away from my family over Christmas? Again, I was shut down. As a matter of fact, Jeremy wanted me to enter the facility the next day. I asked if I could just go home and think about it. To that, he agreed.

Dave and I talked in the car on the way home, and in that brief period of time I came to the conclusion that inpatient treatment was, indeed, the only way to go. I had gone to AA meetings and failed. I had tried to stop drinking on my own and failed. At that point, I had been sober since that fateful Thanksgiving Day, but deep in my soul, I knew it was only a question of time until my impulses took over again. We told the kids that night, explaining what the Ark was and that I would be leaving on Friday, December 5, for thirty days. The irony of how deceiving time can be doesn't escape me. The forty-eight hours of sobriety after Thanksgiving felt like an excruciating lifetime, and now, with my departure looming in that identical space of time, it seemed there was hardly enough time in the world to prepare to leave my family and face the music once and for all.

The kids were a mixed bag of emotions. The younger two didn't fully understand. Britta was sad for me. Erik was grateful. I had the feeling that Erik was almost celebrating the fact that I would be away in addition to getting help. I think he was pretty sick of me by then. My kids were angry and frightened. Erik, as the oldest and the most aware, was really angry at me. And I was angry at myself for letting things get so out of hand. I was also frightened: Would I really be able to stop drinking? How would my family fare without me? Would my family ever accept me again?

I didn't sleep the nights before I left for the Ark. I wish I could recount to you the conversations I had in my head and those I had with

Dave and the kids, but honestly, it's all just a blur because of the alcohol. I suppose the only thing I can recall is the fear I had at the time and that still makes me shudder. There is also a part of me that simply doesn't want to remember because it was quite the nightmare.

I didn't know what to pack for my thirty-day stay, but I figured I wasn't going to be going anywhere. I took one large suitcase filled with comfortable clothes and shoes. Jeremy had warned me that thirty days was the minimum and my stay could be longer. I adamantly said that I would come for only thirty days and no longer. Honestly, I don't know how I packed at all. I was detoxing and feeling quite ill. Later, I was told that stopping drinking as abruptly as I did actually put me at great risk medically. Little did I know the danger of such a precipitous withdrawal. Although, mercifully, I did not suffer seizures, hallucinations, or any profound neurological effects as one can, still, I was a mess.

Once again, Dave drove me to the Ark. He was by my side as I checked in at the office where they took my purse and suitcase and searched them, presumably for contraband. When I walked Dave outside to the parking lot for our good-bye, I just clung to him and sobbed and sobbed. I didn't want to be there. I didn't want him to leave me. I didn't want to leave my family. I was in such enormous pain. To this day, I don't know how I stayed and let Dave drive away. My guess is that deep down inside I knew this was the only chance I had to heal.

When I walked back inside the Ark, a young woman named Heather, another resident, introduced herself as my guide. I discovered that she was only nineteen and had earned the nickname "Snowflake" because she loved the snow so much. She showed me to my room, told me the house rules, pointed out an area where we could keep our own snacks, and showed me the chore schedule for the forty-five current residents who shared cooking and cleaning responsibilities. Then we went right into group therapy, where I was introduced and asked to have a seat while the session continued.

I didn't participate in that first group therapy session. I was too stunned. I was even more astonished when someone entered the room and said, "Jill, give me your cell phone." It wasn't exactly premeditated when I'd shoved it in my pocket earlier. I didn't know it was contraband! As Heather showed me around, I had gone to the bathroom and called Dave and said something like, "Get me out of here." Dave called the Ark and ratted me out. (Apparently one of us was paying attention to the list of contraband.) As a matter of fact, there was to be absolutely no communication or visitors at all for the first two weeks. To say that I handed the cell phone over reluctantly is an understatement. The tears flowed again. I was frightened—and uncertain if I could accomplish what I needed to do: stop drinking alcohol. Forever.

REMEMBER TO DRINK ENOUGH WATER EVERY DAY

Not *everyone* requires exactly eight 8-ounce glasses of water every day. The Institute of Medicine has determined that an adequate intake (AI) for men is roughly three liters (about 13 cups or 100 ounces) of total beverages a day. The AI for women is 2.2 liters (about 9 cups or 74 ounces) of total beverages a day. So the traditional rule should really be stated as "Drink at least eight 8-ounce glasses of fluid a day," because all fluids count toward your daily total.

But there's no doubt that drinking water specifically is important to our overall health and well-being. Water helps to flush toxins and waste products from our bodies. It aids our digestion and keeps us regular. Drinking water prevents dehydration, and it helps us look better, too. Water is proven to help with weight loss and helps hydrate the skin, which in turn reduces the signs of aging. Quite simply, our bodies feel happier and healthier when we consume enough water.

So how do we go about getting enough each day? If I knew exactly how that could be accomplished, I could write a book, it would become a best seller, and I would become a gazillionaire! Oh, wait, I do have some tips here for all of us in *this* book, and they are really good. Okay, I confess . . . I stole these tips from my readers. What can I say? I am terribly neglectful at hitting my daily water quota. Thank you, dear readers and helpers, for the following twenty-three ideas to help us all remember to drink enough water. I plan on trying them all.

- Don't allow yourself a diet soda until you've had two to four glasses of water. Eventually you will find that you won't crave the soda as much.

- Have a big glass of water at every transitional point of the day: when you first get up, just before leaving the house, when you sit down to work, etc.

- Make it convenient—keep a big, insulated water bottle full on your desk and reach for it all day.

- Down a full glass several times a day. Go over to your kitchen right now and fill up a glass. No sipping over time. Just drink it down right after you fill it up.

- Track it. Make a chart and tick it off each time you drink a glass. Do a chart for thirty days and you will have made drinking water a part of your routine.

- Have one glass every hour on the hour while at work or school. When the work/school day is done, your water quota is met.
- Freeze peeled pieces of lemons, limes, and oranges and use them instead of ice cubes—it's refreshing and helps get in a serving or two of fruit.
- After each trip to the restroom, guzzle an eight-ounce glass to replenish your system.
- Set a goal to drink x amount of water a day, then write it down along with your reasons why. Remembering your motivation will help you keep going when enthusiasm fades.
- Every time you walk past a water fountain, take a sip or two. (This is actually advice my own doctor gave me recently after a nasty kidney stone incident.)
- Fizz it up! Get a home seltzer maker like a SodaStream and make your own fizzy H_2O. Add a dash of lemon or a splash of OJ and you'll have a superrefreshing drink.
- Fill up a large cup with crushed ice or ice cubes and snack on them (like candy) throughout the day.
- Make a bet with a coworker to see who can drink more water in the course of a day.
- When drinking juice (apple, grape, or orange) fill half the glass with water or ice and make sure to consume all of it.
- Bring a two-liter bottle of water to work and try to drink it all before you leave for the day. If you don't finish, drink it in traffic on the way home—it's like a race. Use caution if you have a long commute without restroom facilities available.
- Keep a large cup full of ice at your desk and keep refilling it with water. The key is drinking with a straw—you take bigger gulps and drink more at a time.

- Here's a tip (aka mind game to play with yourself) if you're trying to shed some pounds: Let ounces of water double grams of fat. When eating something containing 10 grams of fat, drink 20 ounces of water.
- Drink two full glasses of water at each meal, one before and one after. Also, drink one glass before each snack so you don't eat as much.
- Put reminders into your phone or calendar to drink at regular intervals. Surprisingly, this helps me a *lot*. I know it sounds lame, but I just plain *forget* to drink water.
- Carry a small refillable water bottle at all times and drink during downtime: while waiting in a bank line, sitting on the train, etc.
- Not *all* your water has to be cold . . . drink some of it hot. Have a nice warm cup of tea instead. But be sure it's decaf, since caffeine actually robs you of the water you're trying to drink more of.
- Always keep a bottle of water handy while watching TV, doing laundry, making dinner, etc.
- Add drinking two glasses of water to your daily skincare regimen. Drink, cleanse, moisturize, then drink again.

If you're like me, it might be necessary to use these ideas to *trick* yourself into doing something good for you . . . just until it (hopefully) becomes a habit.

Note: The amount of water that each person should drink daily depends on physical health, amounts of daily exercise, climate, and other external factors (such as pregnancy). Please get advice from a medical professional to find out how much water you should drink daily.

At the Ark, male and female residents were housed in separate buildings. The women had actual rooms, but the men's sleeping facility was barracks-style. I assume that this happened as a result of an outgrowth of space and to keep the two separate. My room was in the basement of the women's building. It consisted of two twin beds with a shared nightstand, two dressers, and a closet. I had a roommate who turned out to be somewhat of a madwoman and ended up leaving prematurely of her own accord. The one positive aspect of her, however, was that she confronted me when it came to my distress. That first night when I couldn't stop crying, she snapped at me and said, "You're here for thirty days and have no choice, so you might as well let it go and just accept it." No coddling from this one.

My second roommate was an eighteen-year-old girl named Ally. She was an absolutely beautiful creature and sweet and fun and bright. I came to truly love her. She also broke my heart. She had so many issues that brought her to the Ark at such a tender age. I kept thinking of my own children and I was so grateful that they were all right. Ally and I were moved upstairs to a larger room with twin beds on opposite sides of the room and our own nightstands. Small shifts in amenities like this made a big difference at the Ark, since the place had become my home—at least temporarily.

Ark residents were awakened at six every morning by the overnight house parent (a nonresident). Kip, a thirty-five-year-old gay man, was my favorite. He typically blasted Lady Gaga or Madonna through the speaker system in the house as our wakeup call. There was something fun about waking up to music that was so lively and upbeat. I'm not sure if everyone else felt as pumped up as I did by the musical selections upon awakening, but to the best of my knowledge, no one complained. I think that Kip's enthusiasm was so infectious and his warmth so encompassing that no one dared to complain. We'd shower, dress, clean our rooms, and then go downstairs for breakfast at seven, where we ate family-style at several tables in one large room. All the residents took meals together in the main house, taking turns with breakfast, lunch, and dinner duty. If it was my turn to make breakfast, I had to get myself up earlier than the others to go downstairs to prepare.

One morning, a male resident, Travis, and I were assigned to breakfast duty. We wanted to make French toast. Travis had his own special twist that I'd never tried before—orange cinnamon French toast. After having that delicious concoction, I have never gone back to plain French toast again. Go figure: one of my favorite recipes comes out of a stint in rehab. Just goes to show that there often is a silver lining.

· orange cinnamon french toast ·

Not only is this dish delicious, it's also simple to make and is perfect for weekday breakfasts as well as entertaining houseguests. We had to make this recipe on a much larger scale than this, but here is a version that should suffice for a family of five.

1 loaf thickly sliced French bread

6 large eggs

Dash salt

⅔ cup orange juice

Grated zest from 1 orange (optional)

2 cups half-and-half

1 tsp ground cinnamon

¼ tsp ground nutmeg

½ tsp vanilla extract

Maple syrup and powdered sugar, for toppings

The night before you want to serve the French toast, slice bread into thick pieces and leave it out to dry. The next morning, beat the eggs and the salt with a fork in a mixing bowl until mixed. (Salt helps break up the yolks.) Add orange juice, zest (if you're using it), half-and-half, spices, and vanilla to the mixing bowl and whisk together.

Preheat oven to 200 degrees.

Soak bread slices thoroughly in egg mixture.

> *Note:* If French bread isn't to your liking, by all means try a different bread, such as brioche or Italian. Just make sure it is very dry and/or stale.

Place as many soaked bread slices in a lightly greased hot skillet as will fit in a single layer. Cook over medium heat until golden brown and no visible liquid egg remains, turning once. Transfer to a baking sheet in a 200-degree oven to keep warm while you cook the remaining toast.

Before serving, dust top with powdered sugar. Serve with maple syrup.

To freeze French toast, cool slices on a wire rack. Place in a single layer on a baking sheet and freeze 1 to 2 hours. Wrap airtight in serving-size portions; freeze up to a month. To reheat, unwrap slices and heat in toaster, toaster oven, or on an ungreased baking sheet in a preheated 375-degree oven for 8 to 10 minutes.

THE ARK WAS A BLEND of tough-love boot camp and comforting nurture. If you didn't follow the rules and do your chores, you lost privileges. The worst privilege we could lose was visitation or outings with family. We had Friday night activities outside the Ark when we piled into the "druggy buggy," our nickname for the big passenger van that transported us to our weekly AA meetings outside the Ark and to our Friday night activities that included things like a movie or bowling. Once we played laser tag. I thought I would die running around that crazy place. As wonderful as the outings were, I missed my family. Imagine if I were playing laser tag with Dave and the kids! The greatest incentive for all of us to never neglect chores was that our compliance with the rules led to permission for family visits. I was my own taskmaster, for sure.

Each morning, there was group therapy, then lunch, and free time in the afternoon when we could read, socialize, and play games. There was a resident there, an attorney, who taught me to play sudoku. Sometimes I just stayed in my room and read. The Twilight series was a best seller at the time, and it was a great escape from the mundane reality of my everyday life. In many ways, this was not only a time of relaxation, but also "alone time" to reflect on and subsequently break bad habits.

Bad habits prevent you from accomplishing your goals, they jeopardize your health—mentally and/or physically—and they waste your time, money, and energy. Here's the theory that I embrace above all: Most of our bad habits are caused by two things—stress and boredom. Anything from biting your nails to wasting time on the Internet to excessive drinking may be unhealthy responses to stress and boredom. Luckily, you can learn to break those habits by substituting positive and healthy ways to cope, and these coping mechanisms eventually become a lifestyle. The *first* step to breaking your bad habit is awareness. Be aware of when they happen and how often they happen. Then you can start to implement some of the following ideas to break them.

HOW TO BREAK BAD HABITS AND START GOOD ONES

Replace bad habits with good habits. It is far too difficult to simply pull bad habits without replacing the needs they were put in place to fulfill in the first place. Giving up television or surfing the Internet might mean you need to find new ways to relax, socialize, or get information.

Remove as many triggers as possible. If you smoke when you drink, then don't go to the bar. If you eat cookies when they are in the house, throw them all away and stop buying them. Make it easier on yourself to break bad habits by avoiding the things that trigger them.

Focus on one habit at a time. If you try to change more than one habit at a time, chances are it won't stick.

Work on establishing one good habit for thirty days. After that time, it has been sufficiently conditioned to become a part of a healthy lifestyle. This positive ritual helps to establish the automatic programs running in the background of your mind.

Join forces with somebody. How often do you try to diet in private? Instead, pair up with someone and quit together. The two of you can hold each other accountable and celebrate victories together. Knowing that someone else expects you to be better can be a powerful motivator.

We often think that to break our bad habits, we need to become entirely new people. The truth is, it's very unlikely you've had these bad habits all of your life. You don't need to quit smoking; you just need to return to being a nonsmoker. You don't need to transform into a healthy person; you just need to return to being healthy. You have already lived without this bad habit, so you can definitely do it again.

Don't punish yourself for being human. Everybody slips up every now and then. Slipping up doesn't make you a bad person; it makes you human. So rather than beating yourself up over it, shake it off and get back on track . . . quickly.

Breaking bad habits takes time and effort, but mostly it takes perseverance. Most people who end up breaking their bad habits try and fail multiple times before they make it work. You might not have success right away, but that doesn't mean you can't have it at all.

Perhaps the most striking aspect of the Ark was the demographic of the residents. There was a musician, a nurse, an artist, a cowboy, a boutique owner, a professional cyclist, a florist, an attorney, three teenagers, and three women who were mothers just like me. I learned really fast that addiction does not discriminate. There is no "type." I was in the minority when it came to my addiction among the women: Most were addicted to prescription medications and some to illegal drugs such as cocaine, methamphetamine, and heroin. But regardless of the substance, all of us there were abusing some sort of drug to numb our pain.

The group therapy sessions could be brutal. There was no room for excuses. People demanded honesty from one another. The group leader and the residents asked questions that targeted aspects of one's personality, forcing us to tackle the issues that landed us there. There was no answer that evoked sympathy. If someone said, "Well, my mother paid no attention to me when I was little," the group took that person to task, reminding them that being an adult means that you've seen enough and lived enough that your past can't be blamed for your present. We were forced to take responsibility for our poor choices and our actions. That was where the real work came into play.

Gloria (left), the founder of the Ark

I recall one group session when our counselor Tracy turned to me out of the blue and said (with regard to the uselessness of excuses), "You can be like Jill, who feels she's living in a loveless marriage." I hadn't said a word about my marriage. It was as though he was psychic. He struck a chord in me. Tracy was quite amazing that way. He'd always listen intently as he sat back in his chair with his fingers steepled, and then he'd come out with something so spot-on. His perceptiveness and listening skills blew me away. I suppose that after years of doing that kind of work, eventually professionals like Tracy could really read people intuitively.

Gloria is the founder of the Ark. She became an addict when she was the mother of five children. They were small when her addiction began. Ah, a familiar story. She ended up going into rehab and righting herself. Around sixty, she and her daughter Laura (in her thirties) were my two counselors for my one-on-one thirty-minute daily sessions. Those sessions, unlike group, were focused on reconstructing me, rebuilding my confidence and self-esteem. Yes, they addressed my addiction, but it was primarily personal therapy that focused on me as an individual outside my addiction. Laura's hero was Miss Piggy for the simple reason that, despite her homely demeanor, she thought she was gorgeous and had what Laura called moxie. Talk about an incentive for self-esteem!

At the end of the second week, Dave and the kids came to visit. I'd made sure to do all my chores and mind the rules. What a beautiful reunion. The kids were comforted and relieved when they saw that the Ark looked like a home. I think they'd pictured an institutional facility that was more like a prison. We hung out in the common area and talked and played board games (Apples to Apples was our favorite) and for just that one allotted hour we had a wonderful time. I introduced them to whomever was in the common rooms at the time, and I think they were also relieved to see that "regular" people were residents. Truly, during my entire stay there, there wasn't one person whom I didn't like. Even my "crazy" first roommate ended up giving me one of the best pieces of advice I've ever received. Dave and the kids left that day with a sense of peace, knowing that I was in good hands. As for me, watching my family drive away without me felt awfully similar to the way it felt back when I first got to Bismarck and realized that I was going to be all right and the homesickness passed. Of course, the circumstances were quite different at the Ark, and the homesickness felt different as well, but I needed to be resilient and see it through. By that point at the Ark, I had detoxed enough that I was clearheaded and feeling better about myself. I also knew that I had to stay at the Ark and let go, and that was tremendous progress on my road to healing.

Life is a balancing act. We are constantly juggling the pressures and demands of work, family, friends, volunteering, etc. Think of it as a four-legged chair that needs all four legs to balance. I like to think of each of those legs as one of four things to keep in balance: health, family, work, and personal growth.

I learned that in order to achieve balance in my life, I had to make some difficult choices that often meant saying no from time to time. For example, if I want to spend more time with my kids, I need to say no to work sometimes. If I want to have more money, I need to say no to spending more often. Finally, I understood that the rewards of balance could be huge. I started to understand how essential it is to spend more time on the things I truly enjoy and less time on unfulfilling activities.

As luck would have it, I got a twenty-four-hour furlough for Christmas because I was in good standing as far as my progress in therapy and execution of chores. I took Heather home with me on Christmas Eve. She was from out of state, and the twenty-four hours left her with no place to go. I didn't want her to be alone at Christmas or back at the Ark. At nineteen, she was like another child for me, and when she met my kids, everyone got along great.

Christmas was amazing. Not just the idea of being home, but the way that people rallied around my family. I was amazed. Our community, church, and neighbors donated presents and money so that Dave could buy presents despite the fact that I wasn't there. Understand that Dave had a lot on his plate as a suddenly single parent with four children and a full-time job. Part of me was slightly crushed that everyone was getting along as well as they were without me; another part was eternally grateful.

Heather and I returned to the Ark on Christmas night. It was bittersweet, but at that point, my time away from the Ark confirmed what I already knew: I wasn't ready for the outside world. I was in a good enough place to know that I still belonged in the refuge of the Ark. I had been so concerned about being away from my family at Christmas, but suddenly I knew that my being at the Ark was the best gift I could have given them.

When my thirty days had passed, I was told that I wasn't ready to leave, and I agreed. If anyone had told me when I first walked through those doors that I would opt to stay after a thirty-day stint, I would have said they were daft. But the Ark, my counseling sessions, my interactions with the other residents, and simply the time I had alone to reflect allowed me to embrace the issues that were deeply embedded within, struggling for resolution. Many of those issues revolved around

my marriage and my broken self-esteem, but there were other compo-
nents of me that made me realize that my alcoholism was no fluke. It
was the result of years of unaddressed issues that were still unresolved
and required my full attention and honesty with myself. In my work at
the Ark so far, I had scratched the surface, but I had yet to arrive at the
heart of the matter. When I got home, I wanted to go home "whole." I
wasn't whole after thirty days. That was quite a confession to make to
myself. But in order to be the kind of wife and mother I wanted to be,
and to make a vow of honesty to my family, I had to be honest with
myself first.

Finally, over a month later, Laura and the other counselors all
agreed that I was ready to move on and face the outside world again.
Rather than feeling elated, I was scared out of my mind. I wondered
whether I hadn't fooled everyone into thinking that I was ready. If that
old resilience in me was a sleight of hand. Yes, I felt different. I felt

My graduation from the Ark

stronger. I felt honest with myself, but then why wasn't I happy or excited to be leaving? Why was I so frightened? Was I afraid that I would not be able to handle the real world and fall off the wagon? I was in a cocoon at the Ark. I had cultivated wonderful friendships with people who were addicts, just like me. There was something about living with several other adults that was kind of nice. I always had someone to talk to and hang out with. It was like being back in college. I worried about going back to being a wife and mother and all my responsibilities. And my job. Would I be able to rejoin the business world without drinking? At the Ark, I was responsible for only myself. Clearly, I was still very fragile.

They have an elaborate graduation at the Ark. You can invite friends and family as with any graduation ceremony. Dave and the children, my parents, and a couple of friends attended. As part of the ritual, residents of the Ark all take turns saying something about you. One thing that really resonated with me at graduation was how many people said that I had made them feel loved and that I was nonjudgmental. I was so surprised. Even people who weren't in my peer group, like the sixteen-year-old drug-addicted skater, said that he felt cared for, loved, and welcomed by me. When the testimonials were over, all of the residents put their hands together and formed a hammock upon which I lay as they cradled me. The lights were dimmed and a song called "Gentle" by Michael McLean played in the background as they rocked me. The lyric that resonated with me the most was: *"We've forgiven and forgotten. We should be more gentle with ourselves."* When I was released from the cradle, everyone circled me into a hug. In my closing remarks, I thanked each person in my family who was in attendance and said that the Ark saved my life along with all the people in there. In particular, I thanked Gloria for creating the Ark and for being such an amazing person. I clung to her, believing that the powerful energy that makes her such a force of nature would get me through even after I was long gone from the Ark.

And so, after seventy-eight days at the Ark, I drove home with Dave and the children. As I told you before, it was my real birthday as well as my re-birthday. We all stopped somewhere for dinner. Honestly, I don't remember where. I'm sure that I blew out a candle, and I can only guess what my wish might have been. When I walked in the door of our home, I felt good, but I was anxious. The Ark had been my security blanket. I was scared to death.

seven

Keeping the Faith

There was no brass band to welcome me when I came home. As a matter of fact, there was barely time to transition as we all walked on eggshells, trying to resume life as we wanted to know it.

That first morning, we all awakened around six-thirty; I made breakfast for the kids, got them off to school, and Dave went off to work. My employer was generous with me, keeping me on payroll for the entire length of my stay at the Ark, but still, I waited a couple of days before returning to work. One thing (among many) that I'd learned at the Ark was how to be kinder to myself. With that in mind, I needed first to ease myself into home, my top priority, and then into work.

Once the kids and Dave were out of the house, I walked from room to room and tried to take stock of what went on while I was gone. To Dave's credit—and, honestly, not without a tinge of chagrin on my part—it was evident that they all managed all right without me. They even had a rotating meal schedule posted with a lot of "breakfast for dinner" nights and a designated "Taco Tuesday." Still, I noticed the absence of my touch and felt a need to reclaim my territory. There was organizing to be done: I cleaned and did laundry. Straightened out drawers and closets, wiped down the refrigerator, went to the supermarket. I have a vague recollection of making a chicken dish that first night, but I can't be certain. The one thing I do recall with certainty is that it was a joyous occasion for me. My prevailing emotions were those of hope and relief. We weren't back to normal, but then again, we had to establish a new normal anyway. I believe that the kids and Dave were on the edge of their collective seat, wondering if they could trust me. I know that I wondered if I could trust myself. It was all an exercise in taking things one day at a time.

HOW TO COPE AND START OVER AFTER ANY BIG LIFE CHANGE

David Foster Wallace once said, "Everything I've ever let go of has claw marks on it." How I love that line! I have always dreaded change. When I went *into* rehab, I dreaded the change; when I came *out* of rehab, I dreaded it again. I think anyone who's gone through a big life change can relate. It's hard to let go of the familiar and embrace the new. Whether you're moving to a new city, leaving for college, or going through some other unsettling experience, there are ways to turn the challenges into growth opportunities. Here are some practical tips on getting through a big life change:

Acceptance

The day I went into rehab, I just couldn't *accept* that I was there. I was only hurting myself by trying to fight the reality of what was taking place. When my first roommate so bluntly stated, "As long as you're here you might as well just accept it and make the most of it," I was stunned into submission. Simple advice, but so profound. I immediately felt a sense of peace come over me. In order to get through difficult change and grow from it, you must first accept the reality that your life will no longer be the same, and try to embrace and look forward to the positive changes that will come from a different life.

One Day (or Ten Minutes) at a Time

Instead of dwelling on an unknowable future, focus your attention on whatever is happening in the present. Learning to live in the now—not in nostalgia for the past or worry about the future—will make any challenges seem more manageable.

Find a Mentor

Talking to others who have gone through a similar transition can make a *huge* difference in helping you to get through yours. That is the whole idea behind Alcoholics Anonymous: to help the addict get through the complete change in lifestyle that is necessary in order to stay sober while knowing that others are there to help them so they don't have to go through it alone. Okay!

Think Positively

Overcoming negative thought patterns and cultivating a positive outlook will shift your mind-set so that you learn to see change as opportunity for growth.

Another Change May Be Just Around the Corner

Once you've dealt with at least one big change, you can take comfort in the knowledge that you can definitely do it again and begin to make macro improvements in your life.

My first night home, over dinner, I told the children and Dave that two of the Ark's exit provisos were that I had to go to evening AA meetings for the next one hundred days and go back to the Ark once a week for six months for a session of aftercare. The kids were not happy that I would be out in the evenings for AA, but I explained the rationale behind it and stated that my attendance at AA was not only a sacrifice for them to make on my behalf, but a sacrifice for me as well to be away from them, and they seemed to understand. They were coming to terms with the fact that I was still in a healing phase. I omitted the fact that I felt almost selfish as I tended to myself, yet I knew that in order to be the kind of mother I wanted to be once again, I *had* to take care of myself almost first or my family would ultimately suffer—again.

AA meetings were essential for me. They took place every night a mere six blocks from our house. Even though the meetings lasted only an hour, many of us hung around and talked afterward. I needed to be around others like me who were in recovery and desperately trying to stay sober. I was still fragile. So fragile, in fact, that despite my stay at the Ark and despite the AA meetings, I had some stumbles along the way when I had a drink. Not to the point where I became drunk, but still. There was one time when I felt particularly precarious and called my counselor at the Ark despite my fear that they would want to readmit me. Instead, they said that my misstep was quite common but that I needed to pull myself together or I would have to go back. Talk about being "scared straight."

Since drinking is no longer an option for me under any circumstances, I have come up with alternatives that can substitute in social situations, or just when a nice refreshing drink sounds appealing. When I discovered this recipe from Simply Scratch for homemade Shirley

Temples, it quickly became a favorite. I was immediately transported back to being eleven years old in Long Beach and going to the bowling alley, where one of my favorite things to do was order a Shirley Temple at the bar. Not only was that a sweet, bubbly treat, but I felt supercool ordering it. It's so funny that after all these years, those memories remain so vivid. The ability that tastes, smells, and sounds have to transport us to another place and time is truly remarkable.

· homemade shirley temple ·

This recipe is adapted from Simply Scratch (www.simplyscratch. com). You may use 7UP or Sprite instead of the sparkling water, but it makes the drink much sweeter. The recipe makes about three cups of syrup. Leftover syrup can be stored in the fridge for up to a month.

32 oz (4 cups) cherry juice

2 cups sugar

Lemon and/or lime sparkling water

Citrus slices (for garnish)

Maraschino cherries (for garnish)

Little paper pennants (just for fun)

Heat the cherry juice over medium heat until it begins to simmer. Continue simmering until the juice is reduced by half. This takes about an hour, but basically, you just "set it and forget it." Remove from heat and add the sugar, stir until dissolved, and then let cool completely.

To mix your Shirley Temple, fill a glass with ice and then add ⅔ cup sparkling water and ⅓ cup reduced cherry juice (more or less to taste) and garnish with citrus slices and maraschino cherries.

If you like, decorate with some cute little pennants that you can make in a couple of minutes using scrapbook paper, double-sided tape, and toothpicks. Be creative! Or you can buy a packet of paper parasols at the supermarket and pop one of those into your Shirley Temple.

PERHAPS ONE OF the most compelling steps in my healing process was revisiting my mom's tenet: "If you're going through a rough time, help others, because then you don't have the time to dwell on what you're going through." As I went to AA meetings, worked, tried to heal my marriage, and took care of my children, I also seized on that. I felt that in AA, particularly, there were (and are) a lot of opportunities to help others as they go through what you go through. Even the monthly aftercare at the Ark presented me with the opportunity to reach out to new residents and reassure them that they, too, could overcome their addictions. My mother, in her infinite wisdom, was so right: Helping others helped me in the process.

FINDING HAPPINESS THROUGH SERVICE (AND GETTING YOUR KIDS INVOLVED)

Those of us who have children know the tremendous amount of effort and sacrifice required to raise them happy and healthy. And yet, despite the sacrifice, I think most of us would say that our kids are one of our greatest sources of happiness. One of my mother's favorite sayings has always been, "You grow to love those you serve." Even if sometimes serving others seems like a thankless job (like motherhood), it remains a reward in and of itself.

Here are some ideas to consider for increasing your service to others, and getting your children involved, too:

Create a Family Culture of Service

Give your kids opportunities to serve others from the time they're young. The younger they start, the more likely they are to continue serving in the future. Parental involvement is critical. If you want to get your children interested in service work, show them how greatly you enjoy it and how important it is to you and the family as a whole.

Lead by Example

Be on the lookout for ways to help someone in need, and your child will take notice. Children imprint: If your habit is to "walk on by," then your child will do the same. In other words, practice what you preach!

Use Your Gifts

Volunteering is a lot less boring if you're doing something you enjoy. An athlete can coach a little league team, and a musician can entertain, for example, at a senior residence. Encourage your kids to help others by showing off their own talents. Doing what they love to do is an easier sell.

Volunteering as a Family Can Be Triply Rewarding— It Accomplishes Three Things at Once

- Your family gets to spend quality time together.
- You're having a positive impact on your community.
- You're teaching your children valuable lessons about service and selflessness.

There are always going to be people in need, and each of us can do something to help someone. Whether our acts of service are great or small, by doing them and losing ourselves in service, we find purpose in our lives.

"One thing I know: The only ones among you who will be really happy are those who will have sought and found how to serve."

—Albert Schweitzer

My mother's advice about helping others inspired me to help myself, as well. Perhaps charity really does begin at home. I tried to change my patterns in terms of being the "perfect" mother and "perfect" homemaker, realizing that perfection is an illusion. I realized that my quest for excellence in my former life nearly all but broke me, and my family, in two. I had to learn to let things go unperfected. All those paintings that might have been hanging crooked on the wall and driving me crazy could wait to be righted. Dinners didn't need to be feasts. Laundry could sit for a day or two. As a matter of fact, everyone could pitch in. Expectations didn't just have to be *of* me, they could be *from* me. And even though it sounds like a small thing, having the kids bring their dirty clothes to the laundry room rather than scrambling around the house for the hamper collection made a difference.

In my absence, Dave became an expert folder, and upon my return, he maintained his job. Kitchen duty changed too, as I cooked dinners and Dave cleaned up. Little things mattered as I strived to let go, tried not to sweat the small stuff, and wanted to give myself a chance to just be Mom and not Supermom. If there was to be hope for me and my family, I knew that I needed to take care of myself first. What they say when you're on a plane about giving yourself oxygen before you administer oxygen to your child became a compelling metaphor for me.

THE THOUGHT PROCESSES learned at the Ark during therapy sessions and my downtime alone were ones that I continued when I came home. I thought about my childhood, when my life was so blissfully sheltered. I considered the irony that in California, as an LDS family, we were a small, tight-knit community in the minority. Living an LDS life was simply who I was and who my family was, and I embraced the fact that we were different. Growing up LDS in California spoke to the aspect of my personality that loved walking to the beat of a different drummer. But here in Utah, the different drummer who summoned me to walk to his beat took me down a bad path.

Once Dave and I moved to Utah, I was suddenly part of an LDS crowd where I lost that sense of individuality and being different. For the first time in my life, being LDS no longer felt special. One would

Me as a child, late 1960s

think that I would have been far more comfortable in a cocoon of like-minded people who were familiar to me, but instead a sense of rebellion boiled in me.

As a working mother in Heber City, I felt like a black sheep when it came to my church and my community. Until we moved to Utah, I adhered to my belief system because I wanted to. Once in Utah, it felt as if there were too many expectations of me. I can't say whether or not my feelings were steeped in reality or just my own intuition, but I felt judged as a working mother when the majority of LDS women stayed at home in their traditional roles. I had a sense that many people felt that I either didn't care enough about my family or assumed that Dave and I didn't have enough money to enable me to stay at home. I was fully aware that even within the confines of my family, I was a pioneer when it came to being a mother and working outside the home. I questioned if the cocoon of my childhood was truly different from the one in which I lived in Utah. I also wondered from where my rebellious spirit emanated. I decided that I was a combination of both of my parents: I had my father's entrepreneurial spirit, which allowed him to start a successful company from scratch, and my mother's nurturing character. I needed to examine my roots and dig into my soul.

As I made a deliberate effort to unearth my inner child, I did not focus on someone who necessarily needed to be healed, but rather someone who needed to take the time to remember the child in her who had been all but forgotten. Of course, I am one of the lucky ones whose childhood memories were largely sweet. For others, looking back may require healing. So when I talk about your inner child here, I'm not talking about something that necessarily needs to be healed or tapped into . . . but rather taking time to remember and cherish that little girl or boy who we haven't thought about or cared for in a very long time. After doing further research on the topic, I discovered even more ways in which we can all benefit from this type of reflection.

REMEMBERING YOUR INNER CHILD

"Every child is an artist. The problem is how to remain an artist once he grows up." —Pablo Picasso

Do you remember what you wanted to be when you grew up? Was it a doctor, lawyer, firefighter, ballerina, teacher? When we were children, the possibilities were endless, and nothing was impossible. When did that all change? And why?

Over the years as we make choices (not all of them good), we lose a little of the joy in life that was so natural as children. We also lose some feelings of the pure hope and belief we have in ourselves. It's hard to be optimistic about the future without that. In my case, the inner voice that once told me good things about myself began to lie to me when I started abusing alcohol. The voice also denigrated me and sabotaged any belief and faith I had in myself and my abilities. As the voice taunted and belittled me, I came to increasingly rely on alcohol to make me feel better. Of course, it was a vicious cycle, as the alcohol only made me feel much worse. As I began to let go of my addictions with the help of the Ark, I had to apologize to "Little Jill" for forgetting her. For not cherishing her. Today, I listen to her, I laugh with her, and I make sure she is a part of my life. I encourage you to find your inner child again.

Here are just a few ways you can start:

Rediscover Your Sense of Wonder

Make a point of paying attention to the world around you. Look closely at a flower or a rock. Marvel at the immense power of a thunderstorm. Go stand out in the rain without an umbrella.

Make Time for Playtime

Think about what "play" means for you and make time for it. I like puzzles, but I rarely ever allow myself time to do one. I need to do more puzzles.

Be Yourself

One thing you can always count on from a child is pure honesty. Adults temper their comments with kindness and consideration, which is a good quality, but don't go so far that you aren't your true self as well. Be a "what you see is what you get" kind of person and respect that in others.

For example, I love to dance. I go to a lot of blogger events where dancing is on the schedule, and even though I immediately raise the median age level on the dance floor by a decade or two, I still will dance the night away when given the chance.

Try Something New

New adventures are pure joy for children, but as we get older, fear of failure holds us back. What's that thing you really want to do but have been holding back on? Take at least one tiny step in that direction.

Embrace Your Vulnerabilities

Crying, admitting fear, and asking for help are all common "childlike" behaviors. But as we grow up, we are somehow made to feel inadequate if we show these types of emotions. Once people get over the fear of how they'll be perceived by others, they often feel more at ease with their lives.

I know these simple techniques won't fix all the stress and sadness in your life, but they can help you rediscover a part of you that may have been missing or forgotten. The innocent child remains somewhere in each one of us.

Back to being LDS in Utah. My religion had always been a lifestyle for me, and suddenly it was a mandate. I will keep reminding you to understand that this is not my excuse for drinking. It is merely a piece of the puzzle that brought me to the crossroads where I took the wrong turn. Drinking and subsequently not attending church were both entirely new (and frightening) sensations for me. There were many times when I questioned why God was taking me down the road I was traveling. I wondered, *Why me?* But I never blamed God. I figured there simply must be a reason for it all.

Although I had stopped going to church, I never abandoned my belief in a Higher Power, and I never felt as though I had been forsaken. Removing myself from the organizational aspect of my religion was never a deliberate action. I never made a statement that I no longer liked the church or had become a nonbeliever. But drinking was not in alignment with being LDS, and I suppose that subconsciously I removed myself from the church community because I felt less guilty that way. There was a point where my addiction was the most powerful force in my life despite my religious beliefs. My lifelong belief in God and Jesus Christ was actually more spiritual than it was ingrained by religion. The problem was not that I stopped believing in God; it was that I had stopped believing in myself. Yet I needed the presence of a Higher Power. Everyone's Higher Power is different, and no one's is the "right" one. For me, it is something that gives me strength, that is bigger than I am. It is out there to help me through the darkest days and nights when no one—not I, not a doctor, not a therapist, not my family—is able to help me.

After I came home from the Ark, I wasn't craving religion, per se, but I was craving something spiritual. Dave and I agreed to disagree about church. I made it clear that I was not necessarily going back. But as I healed, the craving for spirituality intensified. It was an absence in my life that left a gaping hole in my heart and soul. I longed for a Higher Power, something bigger than me to give me strength and a feeling of love and acceptance. It's nearly indefinable, almost mystical. For me, spirituality is something that feeds the soul, and I longed to reconnect with who I was and had become at that point in my journey. I toyed with the idea of going to a nondenominational church that was not LDS, and then it occurred to me, after months of thinking, that all of my touchstones were with my LDS roots, and so I returned.

It really wasn't until I felt stability in myself, in my newly defined roles as woman, wife, mother, and worker, that I was able to physically go back to church. I had reestablished the spirituality within me, but taking it public was entirely different. It was an inauspicious event, really. The kids and Dave had continued to attend church on Sundays, and one Sunday morning, I just got dressed and went with them. Their jaws dropped. There was no fanfare and no stated commitment on my part. It simply felt like it was time.

When I first walked inside, I was nervous. I wasn't worried that people would look at me or judge me—I no longer cared about that—but it felt weird to be back there. I was apprehensive: Would the church still resonate with me as it once had? To my surprise and relief, not only did it feel good to be there, but this time, church provided a new meaning for me. I was there because I wanted to be there, not just because I was supposed to be. It was no longer an expectation, but rather a choice. I took it slowly. After that first Sunday back, I continued to go on most Sundays, but I didn't participate (as I had in the past) in nearly as many social functions.

Now, on Sundays, as I sat in church, I felt like I was home again. I was enveloped in an overwhelming sense of peace. Being back in the church of my childhood gave me a strength that I felt deep in my core, as I felt reconnected to God, someone bigger than me whom I could turn to and rely on. I had a richer appreciation for the belief that we all make mistakes and that's what makes us human. I felt gratitude when it came to the tenet that forgiveness is both divine and Divine. I also took the time to reflect as I sat in church. It was no longer something I did by rote, but rather I really concentrated on being present and quiet and still. The church became a true sanctuary for me. My ability to take that sense of tranquillity home was even more compelling. Although I don't do it as often as I would like, I learned to meditate at home.

As I continue to heal, I find solace in the sanctuary of the church again. As I sit in church now, I feel the comfort that I did when I was a child, when life was innocent and pure.

TAPPING IN TO YOUR SPIRITUAL SELF (IT'S NOT JUST FOR ADDICTS)

Research suggests that people with a sense of spirituality—religious or nonreligious—are likely to experience a greater sense of happiness and well-being. Spirituality can provide us with a sense of connectedness to something bigger than ourselves and give our lives more meaning.

Whether you're just embarking on your spiritual journey or are well on your way, here are a few tips for becoming more spiritual:

Live in Gratitude

Focusing on what you appreciate can help you feel more spiritually connected. Fill your heart with love and thankfulness for all that you have and there won't be any space left for fear or doubt.

Forgive

It's hard to feel connected to the Divine when you're feeling angry, bitter, defensive, victimized, or regretful.

Stop Beating Yourself Up

While you're forgiving others, don't forget to forgive yourself as well. Spiritual living is not about being perfect. We are human beings; we are going to mess up, and some of us quite magnificently. We hurt people; we hurt ourselves. As long as we choose to learn from those mistakes rather than repeat them, then we have a better chance to live a spiritual life.

Let Go

Put faith in the unknown and give up trying to control how your life will play out. When you embrace your spiritual side, you're choosing to believe that God, the universe, or the Divine has your best interests in mind. Trust that there's something positive to be found in every experience and that everything is happening as it should.

Commit to Making the World a Better Place

Whether it is volunteering your time to a good cause, raising money for your favorite charity, or anything else that reaches out, do whatever you can to be of service to others. There is no better way to reach a spiritual high than helping others without expecting them to do anything for you.

Know You're Never Alone

One of the greatest rewards of being spiritual, in addition to general happiness and peace of mind, is the knowledge that you're never alone. There's help on the Divine and earthly levels through support groups, friends, and other resources. Spiritual growth is a birthright of us all. It is the key to a life of happiness and peace of mind.

THERE IS A NATURAL ORDER to everything, and as I came to accept and forgive myself, it was time to turn my focus, once again, to my marriage. I thought about all the things that Dave and I had worked through together. Although I don't like to think that either of us is in any way a victim of a euphemistic "detour," I faced the fact that we were both hurt, scarred, and had endured a great deal of pain. We needed to address our marriage—together. Yes, I was focused on staying sober and, yes, I was fragile, and, no, Dave didn't treat me as though I was made of porcelain. Given all that, I did not want us to be just status quo. We needed to address the breach of trust between us and learn to trust each other again. In that arena, we were both in recovery.

I asked myself what we had to do in order to reinvent our marriage. I had to accept that although our marriage would never be the same, it could be better as it became different. At the core, I knew that we loved each other and that was what I clung to as I recalled our early days when we were head over heels in love. I remembered when we got engaged. That was when Dave first met my parents. We went to California, and my family had one of their traditional beach parties in Dave's honor. During the course of the party, Dave and I slipped off and climbed up on one of the empty lifeguard stands. It was a beautiful evening, and we sat up high, looking over the ocean, our feet dangling over the edge of the stand, and we just kissed and kissed with the ocean playing in the background. I conjured up that feeling and all the imagery surrounding us, when we both felt so lucky and in love. Where were those two carefree people in the lifeguard chair? They had to be in there somewhere. Despite our trials and tribulations, despite my self-perceived loss of innocence, despite the dreams we once had that felt deflated, I clung tight to that day on the beach. I didn't want to have just an okay marriage where we were together for the sake of the kids. I wanted to have a great marriage.

It was as I contemplated all of this that the most extraordinary thing happened: Dave and I made a date, went to dinner alone, and—drum roll, please—told each other what we wanted and needed. I asked him if he would please turn down my side of the bed at night, not just his own. He asked me to please kidnap him and just take him away somewhere. I was floored. But a few weeks later, I did just that— kidnapped him from work, and for just one night, we were away from it all, again, at last. It wasn't quite the lifeguard chair, but it was the beginning of a new beginning.

THE LITTLE THINGS THAT SAY "I LOVE YOU"

I really do firmly believe that it's the little things in life and in relation-ships that are the most meaningful in the long run. I believe that this is the essence of the most successful marriages, relationships, partner-ships, and friendships.

Here is my list of the little things, and I really hope it will inspire you to think of a little thing or two of your own.

- Have your sweetie's favorite snacks on hand. In our house, if there is always vanilla ice cream in the freezer and Spanish peanuts and chocolate syrup in the pantry, the hubster (who has a sweet tooth the size of Mount Rushmore) is a happy camper.
- Honor pet peeves whenever possible.
- Wash their car and put gas in it . . . just because. I know this from personal experience. It's one of my favorite little things that my husband does for me.
- For guys: Watch a chick flick. For girls: Watch a shoot-'em-up movie. Without complaining.
- Grab his or her hand and hold it whenever possible.
- *Very first thing* when you or your sweetie get home from work: Seek out the other person and give them a kiss and a hug. My dad always did this with my mom, and I will never forget it. Not only does this serve to strengthen you and your sweetheart's relationship, it's giving the next generation an example to live up to.

Not long after I made my turn-down-the-bed request, it was fulfilled. Now, each night as I climb into bed, my side is perfectly turned down . . . just like at a fancy hotel. I have to say, when I am practically delirious from lack of sleep (like I am at the end of each long day), I really appreciate this seemingly little gesture more than I think Dave will ever know. Maybe he'll know now.

eight

The Little Things
in a Marriage

Healing a marriage is similar to rebuilding a house left broken by a storm. You start with the foundation and work your way up. Dave and I began by remembering why we loved each other, while admitting that we no longer felt like the same people we'd been once upon a time. Not only did we feel different to each other, we felt different to ourselves. Given all the trials and tribulations that we have been through, we thought we had changed both individually and as a couple. But then we asked ourselves, at our core, had we really changed? For sure, my situation had altered and changed us in ways that were not deliberate and were out of our control, but that wasn't the conscious change that we needed. We decided that we were fundamentally the same people, but we still had a way to go when it came to making changes within ourselves and in the ways that we connected and communicated with each other. As you know, I've never liked change. But as I've gotten older, I've realized the need to embrace it even though a part of me felt like a different person.

I thought about the reasons that made me fall in love with Dave

Dave and me at Britta's wedding, 2013

other than the initial feeling I had when that young, blond, strapping guy walked into the newsroom. I loved his sense of adventure. The fact that he never thought he would marry and settle down, that he would chase storms around the world—and yet I was the one who supplanted that in him. As for me, yes, I always knew I wanted to marry and have kids, but I also wanted to be a career woman. We changed each other's paths. There was a moment that made me pause when I realized that I might have been the greatest storm he ever chased, given what we went through before my landing at the Ark.

I thought about the days after the kids came along. I always loved what a good father Dave was. How he interacted with our children— wrestling on a trampoline with the boys and teasing Britta in the sweetest fatherly way. Playing soccer with them all in the backyard. His ability to discipline them firmly but with kindness. I considered that perhaps he wasn't involved in Kell's diabetes care because he simply couldn't face the disease and that's why the sole responsibility fell on me. Thinking about Dave as a husband and a father was like being on an emotional seesaw. There was the good and the bad, and despite the simplicity of the concept, I couldn't seem to wrap my head around the fact that we are *all* flawed and need to accept one another, warts and all. But there was a lot that I missed. Most of all, I missed the way we used to laugh together. It was painful to realize that we hadn't laughed enough in the last several years. Something so simple meant so much to me and seemed so essential.

For starters, and as trite as it sounds, our first step had to be a willingness to communicate. I can't emphasize enough what poor communicators we were. To think that Dave and I were both communication majors in college! My modus operandi was to retreat into silent mode when I was upset, and Dave's was to ask "what's wrong" questions. It was a bad mix.

We recalled a family session back at the Ark when our counselor asked the six of us to just dump all of our grievances on one another—anything that angered us, bothered us, frustrated us. You name it. It was no-holds-barred. Then she said that all of that debris was going into an imaginary big black garbage bag, tied up tight, and placed in a corner where it would remain unopened for the duration of time. No picking through the trash allowed. That was one sure thing that Dave and I agreed on: There was to be no going back, only forward. I'm the first to admit that's a tough one; forgiving is easier than forgetting. Dave and I recognized that although we went through a honeymoon period after our reconciliation, there were still remnants of intrusions that we left unaddressed. Without opening that bag filled with debris, we had to tackle what remained, toss it away, and start over.

We agreed that going forward we needed to address our grievances as they occurred in order to avoid a buildup. Now, if we disagree about something, we hash it out. We each present our side, and sometimes we agree to disagree and simply drop the subject.

Forgiveness was another essential ingredient in our recipe for healing. First, I had to forgive myself, and I took on a great deal of blame. I suppose my first mistake was allowing myself to be vulnerable altogether when it came to my addiction. I feel as though alcohol blindsided me, and yet I cannot accept that as an excuse for what I feel was a huge mistake when I had that first drink and one led to another and another. At the Ark, I learned that I wasn't responsible for a lot of what happened to me, since addiction is not something one chooses. In spite of that grace, it was hard to forgive myself. I needed to forgive Dave as well, even though his trespasses within the confines of our marriage didn't affect our family the way mine did. I needed to forgive the years that I felt he judged me as my life spiraled out of control. I needed to understand that the reason he clung to religion as I eschewed it was

Dave with Britta and Erik, 1998

that religion became his lifeboat. I needed to understand that he did not shoulder his fair share of parenting responsibilities because that was only what he knew growing up in terms of maternal and paternal roles. I was holding down the fort while Dave was playing in it, and I resented that. I realize now that perhaps he was being the father he never had. Dave has done a complete 180 when it comes to Kell's diabetes care. He nags Kell so much that I have to refrain from telling him to stop. It's a classic example of "be careful what you wish for." Not only does Dave now shoulder aspects of our life together and as a family, he loves the feeling of capability, and we agree that (in part) I hadn't given him the opportunity before.

A WORD (OR TWO) FROM DAVE TO ME

One of the most valuable things I learned through our challenges was that I had to let go of my idea of what the perfect wife and mother should be and I had to give you the time and space to become the kind of wife and mother that you were going to be. When I tried to hold on to a dream, it only caused tension. I came to realize this was never going to help our relationship, and as soon as I let go of the idea of my wife being "perfect," things got much better between us.

Ironically, as soon as I got out of the way and you were free to explore your own creative interests, the qualities that I always wanted in my wife and the mother of my children naturally came along because you were a happier person. You wanted to be the best you could be, but you couldn't do that if you didn't feel good about yourself overall.

The room for growth that we gave each other gave us new ways to appreciate each other. I have a much deeper level of respect for you than when we were first married, not only because of the hard things you have gone through, but also because of the growth and development I have seen come to you as a result.

If I had to identify one thing that saved our marriage, I would have to say forgiveness. It was key to us having any chance to save our relationship. And for me to be able to forgive, I had to ask myself, *Am I really committed to this marriage? Because if I am, then forgiveness has to be the cornerstone.* Forgiveness and trust. The two go hand in hand as far as I'm concerned.

If it was forgiveness and trust that helped *save* our marriage, then it was better *communication* that helped it to heal and continues to nurture it today. While we're still definitely not perfect at it, we're a lot better than we were. We have come to accept that just because we don't agree on everything doesn't make us bad communicators. But if we disagree we still have to be willing to talk about it, which makes for some spirited discussions.

We have made great strides in making each other a priority, and that, too, has been key. It's very easy to become distracted by kids, hobbies, jobs, and you name it. But as long as we remember to put each other first, we just might make it another twenty-seven years.

Dave and I recognized that we had to become a priority for each other—separate from our jobs and our children. We recognized that we had come to take each other for granted. We love our children more than anything in the world, but kids can suck the life out of you! Somewhere along the way, Dave and I got lost. Now, we make it a priority to steal time alone together, and trust me, it's *stealing*. We have date nights where we get a little dressed up and go to dinner. There's something about sitting across the table from each other with no distractions that's just good for the soul of a marriage. Even when I'm away, as I was recently on Valentine's Day, I found a way to be "alone" with Dave. I am fortunate to have a partner who is understanding and cooperative when it comes to our crazy, busy schedules—and we both have them. So, on that particular Valentine's Day, I decided to show just a sliver of my appreciation by leaving a "heart attack" for the hubster.

GIVE YOUR SWEETHEART A "HEART ATTACK"

You will need:

- Several pieces of red and/or pink card stock
- Pencil
- Scissors

That's it. Draw and cut out *lots* of paper hearts. Get your kids to help out (but swear them to secrecy—they will love being in on the fun). You can draw the hearts freehand onto the card stock, or you could trace a heart-shaped cookie cutter. I used a heart-shaped paper punch that I bought at a craft store. I think I ended up making around a hundred hearts.

When you have what you consider to be a sufficient number of hearts,

simply pull back the bedcovers on your sweetheart's side of the bed and sprinkle them all around. Then carefully replace the bedcovers and make the bed look like it hasn't been touched.

That night, when your sweetie climbs into bed, he/she will have a nice little surprise waiting for them that will let them know without a doubt that you are thinking of them. To judge from the hubster's reaction, the "heart attack" was well received.

My daughter, Britta, recently embarked on this journey called marriage that Dave and I have together. I wish I could tell Britta exactly what she should and shouldn't do to make sure her marriage is long and happy and free of conflict or pain. Of course, that's not possible. Everyone has to experience their own journey, pitfalls and all. While I can't tell her how to live her life, or how to ensure her marriage is a happy and long-lasting one, I can share with her at least a few of my own personal secrets to a happy marriage. Secrets learned through trial and error, many ups and downs, and with the help of a few good books.

MY TOP TEN SECRETS FOR A LONG AND HEALTHY MARRIAGE

Give Time a Chance

When I first got married, a long time ago, someone gave me a book titled *Giving Time a Chance: The Secret of a Lasting Marriage*. Many times over the years I have turned to the advice between its covers. Advice that comes from real-life couples who have successfully navigated the sometimes rocky road of marriage. The basic premise of the book is that time

Britta and Neil's wedding, 2013

is a marriage's best friend. If you want to stay and work things out, then time can be on your side. Time can give you security. You fear less that something you've said or done is irrevocable.

When Dave and I were separated and while I was at the Ark, I had a lot of time on my own to think about the history I had with him. I had such conflicting thoughts about it all. While I couldn't imagine continuing on the way we were, I also couldn't imagine going on without him. I was smart enough to know that none of us is perfect, and this particular imperfect man loved my children, our children, deeply, which is a huge factor. Dave and I had built a life and a family together. As shaky as that foundation felt at the time, at least we had it, and that has more value than I was able to previously calculate.

Communication with a Capital *C*

The absence of communication in a marriage can destroy your relationship. Everyone talks about honesty in a marriage, but that's possible only if the lines of communication are open. So even if you're busy with your work, children, gym, household chores, or social activities, set aside fifteen minutes in the day just for your spouse. Use this precious time to sit and talk about something other than just work and family.

Respect

I think we put too much of our emphasis on *love* in a relationship. It's *respecting* your spouse that is equally important in order to strengthen your bond and help your relationship in the long run. Learn to respect each other's feelings and decisions, even if you don't agree.

Compromise

Maybe it's the way we've been conditioned, but a lot of people feel that compromise is a sign of weakness and are often unwilling to do it. But consider the vast number of decisions every couple has to make during the course of their lives as they're faced with situations that require middle ground. This isn't to say that you have to give up on what you believe or think is right. Marriage is not supposed to make all parties feel that they are engaged in one long, endless compromise. Make it more about reaching a consensus or solution with which both of you will be happy.

Sacrifice

True commitment means that you are willing to make sacrifices to keep a relationship alive. The challenge lies in taking steps to maintain the relationship even if you're doing something for your spouse that means you have to give up something for yourself or save it for another time. Both partners in the marriage must be prepared to put their partner's happiness ahead of their own from time to time for the marriage to truly work.

Sense of Humor

Studies reveal that individuals who have a strong sense of humor are less likely to experience burnout and depression and are more likely to enjoy life in general, not to mention their marriage.

Keep Dating

Dating your spouse is one of the most important forms of marriage maintenance. It helps you reconnect and reminds you that you married this person as an individual and not just to be a co-parent. Dating also creates variety and interesting experiences in your life that make new memories and continue to strengthen your relationship and add to your shared history.

Commitment Is Crucial

Before committing to marriage, be certain that your values and life goals line up in the first place so that your marriage doesn't forever seem like one big exercise in compromise.

After you are married, it's important to take a long-term view. It's kind of like investing in the stock market: Don't pull your money out as soon as it takes a dip. You and your partner are a package deal. You have to take the good with the not so good. Recognize that marriage is a journey that ebbs and flows. Have faith that although passion can wane, it can also reignite over time and sometimes when you least expect it.

Acceptance

This might be the best-kept secret to a long-lasting and happy marriage. Spending all your time trying to change your partner or perfect those annoying little traits will bring nothing but disappointment. You fell in love with the person in front of you. Staying in love is up to you.

This brings me to one of the most important secrets of a long-lasting marriage, and one that has seen me through many rough patches over the years.

Remember Why You Married Each Other

Always remembering what it is about your partner that drew you to them will make certain that you never forget your love for your partner. It ensures that he remains beautiful in your eyes. Many things may change throughout the course of your marriage, but the one thing that will always remain is the reason you fell in love in the first place.

nine

The Green Chair

After the Ark, life became all about healing. As I healed, Dave and I continued to reconstruct and the kids embraced a new perspective. I was an addict in recovery, and although I kept in touch with her, I was a long way from that ambitious and innocent little girl in California whose every dream was certain to come true. I had to keep myself in constant check and be true to myself. I longed, if you will, for my salad days, when life was so innocent and troubles on the horizon were not even imaginable. This led me to thinking about food (something I think about often—don't we all?), and one good thing then led to another. My mind tossed salad and I recalled Yeats: "It's certain that fine women eat a crazy salad with their meat." I realized that I could still be the woman I wanted to be, but only if I eased up on myself and made my life simpler.

"CRAZY" SALAD IN A JAR

Premade salads in a jar are a great option for school and office lunches, picnics, and even at-home lunches. They are easy to grab and go and are a healthier option than most portable foods. The salad dressing can be added right in the jar, and when the ingredients are packed correctly everything stays crisp and fresh.

A Few Tips for Creating a Delicious and Lasting Salad in a Jar

> Start with a clean widemouthed jar that is completely dry. Moisture is not your friend when assembling a salad.
>
> Tear—don't cut—lettuce, to keep the edges from turning brown.
>
> Start with the dressing at the bottom, and keep the greens from coming in contact with it.
>
> Place items that'll soak up and marinate in the dressing as the next layer for the best salad flavor.
>
> To make the salad a little heartier, try adding a protein, like chicken, quinoa, or beans.
>
> Pack the jar full. Not only does this give you the most veggies for your space, but it also helps keep things from shifting and moving around if it happens to tip over on its side.
>
> A pint mason jar full of salad makes for a perfect-size workplace lunch. If you want to go for a big, entrée-size salad, use quart-sized jars.
>
> Keep the ratio approximately half toppings, dressing, and proteins, and half greens.
>
> Place a piece of folded paper towel on top of the salad, before the lid goes on, and it will absorb the excess moisture and keep the greens crisper.
>
> To eat, either dump it all into a bowl or eat it directly out of the jar. Shake the jar first to distribute the dressing, and then dig in.

.   .   .

BEING BACK AT WORK was challenging. For one thing, it took a concerted effort to avoid the triggers that could set me back, like work-
related gatherings where people stood in a circle, chatting away with
drinks in their hands. My drink of choice was Diet Coke. Sometimes I
wondered if people thought I'd slipped a little rum in it. I occasionally
felt insecure about being the nondrinker and wondered if people who
didn't know me were wondering why I wasn't drinking. Temptation
was rampant and nearly demonic. Really, the only place I felt safe was
at home. But I knew I couldn't stay home forever. I needed to create a
new me. I knew that would be a slow evolution. I made no pronounce-
ment that "Things are going to change around here!"

It was a daily exercise for me to see light at the end of the tunnel.
For sure, it took a good year for all of us to establish a sense of mutual
trust where the kids felt they didn't have to walk on eggshells around
me and I felt they could believe in me. I also needed to believe in them
insofar as not having to spend each day of my life proving that I was
capable of sobriety. It took a lot of physical and emotional energy and
effort. Nevertheless, I wasn't trying to win anyone over by being my
former supermom-self. I was no longer a slave to the stove even when
we weren't planning to go out for dinner. As I was picking up the pieces
of my life after rehab, I realized I had to be easier on myself in many
ways. Now, this may sound silly, but my new best friend became my
Crock-Pot.

As a matter of fact, I learned to love my slow cooker. I searched for
and found lots of great slow cooker recipes online and even reworked
some old favorites to be Crock-Pot friendly. The benefit was twofold: I

didn't have that nagging concern all day about what I was going to make for dinner, and it saved me money because I wasn't running out for fast food at the last minute before a hunger revolt erupted. Plus, it's so nice to come home to the divine smell of a delicious dinner cooking.

EMBRACING YOUR SLOW COOKER

Slow cookers have *slowly* been making their way back into popularity the last few years. They're not the flower-covered stoneware our mothers used, and they have lots of fancy features now, but the appeal remains the same. Set it and forget it. All it requires is a little preplanning and a few extra minutes in the morning to throw it all together.

Here are two of my favorite recipes:

best (and easiest) pot roast recipe ever!

1 pot roast

1-ounce packet of dry brown gravy mix

1-ounce packet of dry au jus mix

Water

Cornstarch (for the gravy)

Place roast in Crock-Pot and sprinkle both packets of dry mix over the top. Add water until it is halfway up the side of the roast and cook *low and slow* for 8+ hours. If desired, you may also add some of your favorite vegetables to the pot. No adjustments needed.

The "low and slow" cooking method practically guarantees a fall-off-the-bone roast . . . and the combination of the gravy and au jus mixes makes *delicious* gravy after the roast is done.

To make the gravy: Pour juice drippings into a saucepan, add about a cup of water, heat to boiling, and thicken with a mixture of cornstarch and water. Boil for a minute or two and you are done. The gravy train has reached its destination!

copycat cafe rio shredded chicken

6 chicken breasts

½ cup zesty Italian dressing

1 tsp minced garlic

11-ounce package dry ranch dressing mix (mixed with ½ cup water)

½ tbsp chili powder

½ tbsp ground cumin

Place all ingredients in a Crock-Pot. Cook on high for 5 to 6 hours *or* on low for 8 hours. Shred with a fork and serve. This chicken is great in tacos, burritos, salads . . . you name it! Just add cheese, lettuce, sour cream—all the usual suspects—and enjoy.

You can also double or triple this to make extras for freezing. Then simply thaw and reheat for a lickety-split meal.

.   .   .

IT'S NOT AN EASY TASK to change or attempt to defy the personality you're born with. I tried to let go of the obsessive little things I felt obliged to do on a daily basis, but as I did, there was still something missing. It was that old "I want more" rearing its head. I needed to find the passion that we talked about during my stay at the Ark. My counselors had told me, almost warned me, that when I stopped drinking and reentered the world as a sober person, I would have to find something that would fill what would feel like a void in me. My job at the phone book company was becoming increasingly unfulfilling. And, of course, I felt guilty as I considered leaving for another pursuit, since they had been so generous and kind to me during my stay at the Ark, keeping me on payroll and holding my position for me. But I remembered to give myself the oxygen first.

I knew two things were true: I loved to write (as passionately as I had when I was a child) and I wanted to help others and give back. Both were vaguely intertwined concepts in my mind, but something was lingering there, waiting to happen.

There is and will always remain a green leather armchair and matching ottoman in our living room. The set originally belonged to my sister Rebecca, but they've been ours for about eighteen years. One night, about six months after I returned to work at the phone book company, when the house was finally sleeping, I cozied up in that chair with my laptop. I got on Facebook, like I usually do at the end of the day, to check up on my "social life" and share thoughts and ideas that I just had to put down *somewhere*. But I worried that my stream of consciousness in the news feed was becoming quite the bore to my Facebook friends. What I really needed was a better forum. I

The green chair

decided that night to start my own blog and share my "good things" there.

There was a website, www.blogger.com, where people could start their own blog for free, so I set up my blog site. I knew how to navigate the Blogger website, my knowledge tapped from the days when I taught myself HTML and when I posted on couponing websites under the name "Jillee" (not only because *Jilly* and *Jill* were both taken but also because my dad's nickname for me when I was a little girl was "Jilly Bean"). I also wanted to post something each night that spoke to what we all did at the Ark as we focused on one good thing at the end of the day. With that in mind, www.onegoodthingbyJillee.com was born. The name for the blog was conceived in about three minutes after a conversation with myself that went something like this:

"Okay, smart girl, what are you going to blog *about*?" I asked.

"I'm just going to post one thing a day that I think is interesting and/or helpful and pass it on to others so that maybe they will think it's interesting and/or helpful, too," Smart Voice replied.

This simple, fundamental mission immediately reignited the love affair I'd had with writing since I was a little girl.

My first blog post was called "In My Spare Time" (get it?), and I used it as a jumping-off point from which I could introduce myself to a potential new audience. My original audience consisted of my family and a handful of friends. I wrote solely for the sheer enjoyment. I was also inspired as I recalled my production days on *Good Things Utah*.

I had no specific idea of the direction that the blog would take and just wrote spontaneously about whatever had struck me on a certain day—whether it was something beautiful I saw in a shop, something I read, or something I thought about. For sure, I had no idea that the blog would take on a life of its own and attain the reach it ultimately did. All I knew was that I was determined to sit down in that green chair each night and write something good at the end of the day. This activity has allowed the new me to take control of my life in a positive way. I was a new person who, merely two years before, might have sought solace in a box of wine, and this time I took solace in my childhood joy of writing. It was most empowering.

HOW TO QUIT A JOB GRACEFULLY

Turning in your resignation isn't easy, regardless of whether you love or hate your job and your reasons for quitting. First of all, be sure that you really do want to quit. Then, handle your resignation carefully. A bad exit can have long-range consequences.

Here's a list of ways to quit a job gracefully:

Do It in Person

Your boss should be the first person in the office to know that you're quitting. Tell him or her in person and make sure that it comes straight from you and you only.

Give Proper Notice

Be sure to offer your employer at least two weeks' notice when quitting. Usually, the more time your company has to find your replacement, the better, but anywhere from two weeks to one month is standard.

Write a Resignation Letter

The resignation letter is for your records and the company's records, so keep it brief and professional. You need to include only the fact that you're leaving and the date of your last day. The reason is unnecessary—leave it out.

Train Your Replacement

If there is time, offer to train your replacement. It's a generous act of kindness and leaves your reputation in good standing regardless of the circumstances under which you are leaving. It also ensures that you can give your work the best chance of being done well in your absence, which will do wonders to maintain the goodwill you've already worked so hard to establish.

Don't Just Walk Out

No matter how bad things may seem, walking out unannounced is rarely a good idea. The last thing you want is to have a bad reputation follow you out the door, and leaving without a word will nearly guarantee that you leave everyone—not just your direct supervisor—with a bad taste in their mouths.

Keep Up the Hard Work Until the End

It's easy to start slacking off as soon as your job has an expiration date, but that's unfair to your coworkers. Finish all projects and tie up loose ends.

Leave the Door Open a Crack

If you've done good work, there is no reason you couldn't come back later, when things for you and for the company might have changed. Don't close any doors permanently.

Ask for a Reference

Before you leave, ask for a letter of recommendation from your manager. As time passes and people move on, it's easy to lose track of previous employers. With a letter in hand, you'll have written documentation to give to prospective employers.

Don't Forget the Details

Find out about the employee benefits and salary you are entitled to receive when you leave. Inquire about collecting unused vacation and sick pay, and keeping, cashing in, or rolling over your 401(k) or other retirement plan.

Keep in Touch

Your farewell e-mail should be friendly but to the point: Tell your coworkers where you're going, where you can be reached, and that it was a pleasure working with them. Encourage them to keep in touch, since you'll probably run into one another again, especially if you remain in the same field.

Above all, don't burn any bridges. Leave on a good note. Your employers should be sorry to see you go.

Roughly six months after starting my blog, employing all of the advice I mentioned, I quit my job. It had come to a point where I felt that my bosses and I did not see eye to eye. I felt undervalued and unappreciated, and although they had been wonderful to me during my stay at the Ark, it was time to move on in that arena as well. I gave my notice, stating that I would stay on until they hired someone else. After a month, with no one on the horizon to replace me, I said I simply could not stay any longer.

With One Good Thing by Jillee, I knew that I had found a passion in the blog as well as within myself. I knew that I was on to something.

ten

Dreams Can Come True

My family thought I was slightly crazy staying up until the wee hours of the morning doing a "silly blog." But as I sat in that cozy green chair, in front of the picture window that looked out over the panoramic view of Mount Timpanogos against a midnight-blue sky (lit by the moon, if I was lucky), I was in pure heaven. At first, I couldn't explain to my family why I was doing what I was doing, since I wasn't exactly sure myself. All I knew was that I thoroughly enjoyed it and it brought me a sense of peace as well as purpose.

Have you ever stopped for a moment to think, *What is my purpose in life? What is my passion?* I think we've all struggled with that question at some point in our lives. Especially as we mature and "real life" kicks in and our "purpose" seemingly becomes more about bills, mortgages, and mouths to feed than pursuing the work that we love. It wasn't until I was in my forties that I seriously contemplated that question. As I sat and blogged, my purpose was forming right before my eyes.

EXERCISES FOR FINDING PURPOSE AND PASSION IN LIFE

Make a List of People You Admire

Think of all the people you know personally or whose inspirational success story you've heard about, whose career you would most like to emulate. (I think of people like Steve Jobs, Oprah Winfrey, and J. K. Rowling.) Read *everything* you can about them to find out how they got where they did, or if you know them personally, see if you can set up a meeting to "pick their brains." This is one reason that reading biographies is such great fun.

Examine the Themes in Your Life

Look at your collections, the magazines you like to read, the music you listen to—even your credit card statements. Notice any recurring themes? Notice what subjects you are already gravitating toward and in what areas you are spending the most time, money, and energy. Those are good indicators of where your passions lie and the direction you should be heading.

Remember What You Loved as a Child

Often our truest passions emerge in childhood, only to be snuffed out by real-life pressures. As early as elementary school I loved to write. It was my very favorite subject in school and the one in which I always excelled. Think about what you loved long before you had to worry about your family or career or bills. I cannot be more emphatic about the importance of getting back in touch with your inner child.

Complete These Sentences

If I had no possibility of failing, I would . . .

If money were no object, I would . . .

Ask Your Friends

Sometimes we're just not the best judges of what makes us happy. Ask people who know you intimately what appears to make you happiest and enthusiastic. Their answers given with objective insight are often quite surprising and enlightening.

Believe It Is Possible!

People often don't pursue their passions because they don't believe it's possible. As someone who finally dared to live my dream, I can tell you with certainty that anything is possible. Uncovering your life's passion is one of the most important and life-altering endeavors you will ever undertake.

Quit Talking and Start Doing

Build your life around what you love. It is something you'll never regret.

I feel very fortunate that I was able to identify and pursue my passion, and these tips still serve me well. Doing what I love means I'll always be employed but I'll never have to work.

As the nights wore on and I continued to write, I was struck by my newfound confidence, and as a result, my abilities began to return and subsequently strengthen. When I commit to something, I give it my all. One hundred percent! So, from the night that I posted "In My Spare Time," regardless of how tired I might be, how difficult a day

I'm having, as close to impossible as it feels to write, I put pen to paper (sort of) anyway. And I have yet to miss a single day. In the beginning, I had to get up very early—for my day jobs at the phone book company and with the kids—and stay up very late, but it was worth it because I loved my night job so much.

Blogging became a preferable addiction—one that had no adverse consequences, and yet it did alter my mood because it gave me a shot of pure elation. When I clicked "publish" and finally shut down the laptop, I felt completely satisfied. I had fulfilled my intention and completed my day. I felt good about what I had written and the fact that it might connect with other people. As I left the green chair and readied for bed—and it was tempting to just curl up in that chair and sleep— my brain felt rested and unencumbered by thoughts that once might have me otherwise restless. I was tired, but it was a good tired, and I slept well and soundly. In the beginning, One Good Thing by Jillee was simply for me. I never even *entertained* the thought that one day it could be something that would replace a "real job," let alone become one. It was just about finding the solitude I needed in order to get back in touch with myself.

FIND YOUR QUIET PLACE

My house is rarely quiet. Even during the school year, it seems there is always *someone* around making a racket. Whether it's one of my boys who's home sick, the hubster home "sick," my daughter or daughter-in-law milling about or working for me as they do now, or myriad other folks who come and go from this house . . . it's rarely, if ever, quiet.

I've come to accept that noise and commotion are an unavoidable part of my life, and to be honest, I wouldn't have it any other way. So how do I manage to get work done? I use a few techniques to find the quiet place I need to be productive.

Create Solitude

Designate one room of your house as a noise-free zone where family members (and this includes you) can go relax. And no cell phones allowed!

The Sound of Silence

Earplugs are a great tool when you absolutely, positively have to concentrate and you are surrounded by noise. (Earplugs also work well when you sleep with a snorer.) Pop them in and create a bubble of serenity around you. They're portable, cheap, and available everywhere.

Keep the Peace

Find the most quiet or peaceful time of the day in your home and take advantage of it to steal moments for yourself. (And this doesn't mean cleaning or doing laundry. You can do those another time.)

Get up early or stay up late, if necessary. The only truly quiet time in this house is between eleven p.m. and six a.m. Since I don't want to get up at four a.m., I stay up until one a.m. It's six of one, half a dozen of the other when you think about it. Either way, I'm tired. But it's the only time I can get things done that require complete concentration. I need peace and quiet. So I do what is necessary to get it. I'm learning to power nap, though.

Television Can Be the Devil

Okay, perhaps this is a bit overstated, but I got your attention, didn't I? Television can be a nice stress reliever when you're not working, but never turn it on when you're trying to get work done. It's a distraction with a capital *D*. Turn it off. Or leave the room if you have to. Hell, get rid of it altogether if necessary!

Have an Escape Route

The bathroom is your friend. An oasis of quiet, the bathroom can give you the alone time you need for a break when there's just nowhere else to go. This advice is best taken advantage of when there isn't a line of people waiting for you to be done.

I smile to myself when I think back to the little girl in me who wrote "A Day in the Life of a Piece of Chewing Gum." Talk about the writing being on the wall. I felt such emotion as my "silly blog" helped me to reconnect with the touchstones in my life that had been forgotten. My family was right—I was crazy. Crazy in love with writing.

Through this outlet, I became whole. In one corner of my heart was the writer, and in another was the homemaker, and it struck me that they could truly occupy the same place. After I quit my job at the phone book company, when the blog was just more of a fulfilling hobby than anything else, I still viewed it as a job (that didn't pay well) and defined myself as someone whose main purpose in life was making a home for Dave and our children. Creating a beautiful space where we can all live and thrive, where it's warm and welcoming and there is good food on the table and decorations during holiday times and special occasions, was my greatest priority. And perhaps for the first time in my life, neither I the writer nor I the homemaker felt at risk of being displaced. I came to realize that making a home filled with love and devotion is really the stepping-stone that makes everything else all the more worthwhile. Epiphanies often come from suffering through trials and tribulations—at least, they did in my case. There was a time when I carried the burden of dissatisfaction so heavy on my shoulders. Blogging each night about one good thing allowed me to embrace all the facets of myself and have the best of both worlds.

EMBRACING (AND REDEFINING) THE ART OF BEING A HOMEMAKER

My mom was the quintessential homemaker when it was still cool to be a homemaker, back in the fifties and sixties when Ozzie and Harriet were the role models on television. In the seventies, eighties, and nineties, however, the titles of "homemaker" and, for sure, "housewife" took a beating, as more and more women got jobs outside the home. In recent years we seem to have come full circle; both men and women are realizing that women (and men) with full-time roles as homemakers also have a demanding job and long hours.

Although homemaking has regained some of its previous status, there are two major differences. Even though elective homemaking is hard work, people take pride and pleasure in what might have become a lost art. In addition, it is no longer solely a female role. The plain truth is that even in the smallest of towns, very few of us need to bake bread, can our own jams, pickle our own cucumbers, or make our own cheese. Rather, we pick and choose projects that bring us pleasure and satisfy us.

Being a homemaker no longer has to be a full-time job as it was in our mothers' era. One can work outside the home and still be a homemaker at the end of the day. Even when both parents work outside the home. The beauty of being a homemaker in the twenty-first century is that it is à la carte and we can pick and choose based on the individual needs of everyone in the home.

Homemaking has been redefined as we use our instincts, creativity, and skills to nurture the people and things we love (including ourselves). I am proud to call myself a working mom and homemaker.

From the very beginning, I simply wrote about anything that struck my fancy during the day. Even just a thought that briefly danced in my head that I then jotted down on a slip of paper so I'd remember it later that night. Perhaps I read an article on a latest trend or a passage on some theory or philosophy that struck a nerve in me. Sometimes I'd be at a store and I'd have a bright idea for a recipe or a homemade beauty product or simply a way to cut costs when I wondered why everything was adding up so much at the checkout. My blog runs the gamut— from chasing down bargains to chasing down the more meaningful things that we also love; from a mandarin coriander hand wash I came upon in a sweet little store to waxing on about life in general. In other words, I have no specific platform in mind. It isn't geared to crafts, cooking, lifestyle, cost-cutting, or any of the other typical blog categories. It is a potpourri of all good things.

My desire to have an eclectic website and blog grew from two things. First of all, I can't stop thinking! My fascinations are all over the map. The second reason is more like a confession: When it comes to crafting, I'm no Martha Stewart. I never got into scrapbooking. I don't have a lot of ongoing projects involving glue guns, yarn, beads, fabric, etc. I admire those who are crafty, and although I don't consider myself crafty, I do consider myself to be resourceful, imaginative, and creative.

Before I throw anything away, I look at it to see if I can find any other use for it. I recycle what I can. With the explosion of the online craft world and that addicting little thing called Pinterest, it's easy to become so overwhelmed by all the amazing ideas out there that we feel like inadequate crafters. But I'm a firm believer that everyone is capable of creating something.

THREE TIPS FOR THE NOT SO CRAFTY

- Resist the urge to do every craft that catches your eye. Decide if it's something that you really want to try and if you want to spend the time and money required to do it.
- Start small. If you want to learn to knit, don't start off by attempting to make that full-length sweater coat you saw on Pinterest or in the window of the yarn store. You'll only end up with a serious case of frustration. Instead, pick up a basic knitting book, buy some yarn, and learn how to knit a few rows first. Then try a simple scarf. Baby steps.
- Ask your crafty friends for help or sign up for a class. Sometimes a little moral support and the knowledge that there are other less crafty folk out there is all it takes to get you going.

And you thought you weren't crafty!

As I happily blogged along, I wondered how many readers I had. On Blogger, there are these little widgets that you can install, and one is a counter that measures traffic to your website. So, I added the widget to my blog, and if my page was open, I could hear a click and see when the widget counted another reader.

My first indication of traffic on the blog was four months after I began blogging. I had a thousand visits in one day! I was shocked. Prior to that point, I had an inkling that I had some readers, but never expected that many. So, I Googled how to sign up for Google ads, thinking, *Hmmm, maybe I can actually make a few bucks from this blog.* Back then, anyone could put a Google ad on their page. A Google ad is based on what people view in their browser. The process has since become slightly more complicated but is certainly doable. Now you have to apply to Google AdSense and be accepted before you receive the code that allows readers to see the ads.

There is no demographic analysis. As part of the ad code that's embedded on your page, Google builds an ad based on the cookies on the viewers' pages. For example, if you have searched recently for shoes or furniture, you might see an ad appear on your page from Zappos .com or Wayfair.com. Google did the analysis, and for my x number of visits, I'd get x amount of revenue from the ad. The revenue from the Google ads was minimal—maybe twenty-five to fifty dollars per month—but it was still more than I had ever anticipated, clueless as I was in the beginning, when I had no idea that you could make money from a blog. In addition, I started getting comments. People were actually interested in what I had to say and post. This further fueled my desire to make it even bigger and better.

The little widget began to move faster and faster. There were times when I stole a moment to check on it during the day and heard a click every four seconds. I ended up switching from Blogger to WordPress .com, as the Blogger widget was so overloaded with visitors that it stopped working. Besides, WordPress's platform, the forum used by most professionals, offered better opportunities for customization, and by that time, I was putting more and more graphics and photos on my pages.

I will never forget the Sunday afternoon that I was at my mom and dad's house and as my mom and I sat in the kitchen watching the counter, it surpassed 900,000 page hits! I realized the magnitude of it all and, frankly, I was stunned. Maybe this was something more than just one good thing that I was doing for myself at night in my green chair. I had no idea that by feeding my soul, I'd end up with a feast. I was suddenly faced with a whole new frontier that turned out to be way beyond my wildest dreams.

I was also working long hours—much longer than ever before. This was surely a casualty born out of working from home, which can be most deceiving. In a lot of ways, working from home is harder, because your home is your office and you no longer have the respite that the physical separation can often afford. One of my biggest challenges still is being able to unwind and simply relax at the end of the workday. I know that all work and no play makes Jill a cranky girl, so I try to make a concerted effort to unwind at the end of the day.

I find it is especially helpful—difficult as it may be—to turn off technology. You can't unwind if you have e-mails arriving on your phone every two minutes. I just power everything—the phones, laptops, tablets, you name it—right on down. The world will not end if we take some time out. I often need to consciously remind myself of this fact. This is also a great time for pleasure reading. No business, papers, or reports—*nothing* to do with work. Read a novel that is going to transport you to another world, or pick up a beautiful travel book and start dreaming about your next vacation.

I really do believe it's important to find ways to decompress after a hard day at work. It is important to consciously stop your brain from thinking about work and instead focus on all of the other wonderful things that are going on in your life. There will be plenty of work left when you return there in the morning.

eleven

Family Ties

The response to One Good Thing by Jillee was startling to me to say the least, and it also gave me a good idea of what people were hungry for, so I did my best to feed that hunger. My experience as the producer of a daily talk show proved to be a great asset in being able to gauge what would work and what wouldn't on a day-to-day basis for the blog. All those years of writing snappy headlines and juggling and identifying popular topics were paying off in a big way. As the number of visits continued to climb and ad revenue began to increase, I knew that I had found my new day job, and quitting the job at the phone book company felt truly right for the first time.

You might say the blog's early success could be attributed to my relentlessness, the explosion of social media, or simply the fact that people, including me, were eager for smart ways to make their lives easier, safer, more frugal, and less wasteful. Ideas are constantly coming into my head like little explosions. For example, one day my sister came over to visit and found me putting dots of yogurt on a baking sheet and then placing the sheets in the freezer. Convinced that I was losing it, she still humored me when I asked her to take a couple of pictures of my "invention" with her camera phone. This would be the beginning of my second-most pinned picture on Pinterest, that now ubiquitous photo-sharing bulletin board. Frozen Yogurt Dots became a runaway hit on both Pinterest and my blog, and so began a run of "good things" that still live in infamy on the World Wide Web. The second blog post to hit big was bringing new life to old cookie sheets, closely followed by how to get rid of yellow armpit stains. You'd think I'd discovered electricity rather than just a way to save your favorite white T-shirts from the trash.

FROZEN YOGURT DOTS

I am fairly obsessive about food. Oh, who am I kidding? I'm fairly obsessive about everything . . . but food especially. A couple of my food obsessions are *anything* that contains lemon and (almost) anything that's frozen. I have a weakness for frozen treats, so when I had the idea for freezing little dots of yogurt on a cookie sheet, I knew it was made for me. The beauty of this frozen treat, as opposed to the dozens of other frozen treats I have pinned to "My Frozen Treats Obsession" board on Pinterest, is the simple preparation. I was pretty sure that even my picky eaters who don't like the yogurt with fruit pieces mixed into it would like these plain or flavored dots. And I was right. They ate them like candy. After all, they look like they *could* be candy. But they are frozen, creamy deliciousness. *Much* better and healthier than candy (or ice cream).

How to Make Frozen Yogurt Dots

- Take a resealable plastic bag and put it inside a tall water glass, with the top of the bag folded over the rim.

- Fill the bag with approximately one cup of your favorite yogurt. With scissors, snip a tiny piece off one corner of the bag.
- Squeeze tiny dots of yogurt in several lines onto a cookie sheet and then place the sheet in the freezer.

These freeze superfast, so if you're in a hurry for a frozen snack, pop some dots in the freezer and in less than an hour you'll be enjoying your own delicious creamy treat.

I was working day and night, but it hardly felt arduous. I was pumping so much adrenaline that I could have been running track. Finally, the amalgam of my professional and domestic lives was exactly the one I had once only dreamed about and wished for, and it all happened so fast. Although I wasn't keeping track of time, it was roughly nine months after I started the blog that it held all the hallmarks of becoming a successful *business*.

That was when my exceedingly entrepreneurial thirty-four-year-old nephew, Scott Warner, got wind of what was going on. Apparently, the updates on traffic that I gave to my parents and siblings made their way to him and a lightbulb went off in his business-oriented brain. Scott is, and always was, a natural-born salesman. As luck would have it, he was also fascinated by blogs in general and, as one who has his ear to the ground for opportunity, he was convinced that there was something brewing with One Good Thing. Scott gave Aunt Jill a call.

Scott's call could not have come at a better time. As exciting as the success of the blog had become, I was starting to feel overwhelmed. The pace at which things were happening and the ways in which everything was getting "out there" were becoming nearly too much for me to handle. I had to face the fact that a younger generation (Scott's) had the edge over my own when it came to navigating the labyrinth that is the business of blogging and the explosion of social media. Scott said that I was "onto something big," and although I wasn't quite sure if I believed it myself in terms of exactly how "big," I deferred to him, excited and quaking in my boots at the same time. I was getting 40,000 visits each day at that point, but that number was *still* nearly impossible for me to compute and trust. I was nearly bruised from pinching myself.

NO-NONSENSE TIPS FOR BLOGGERS

- Content is king. Quality content should be your top priority.
- Learn how to take pictures.
- Learn how to do social media.
- Learn at least a little HTML.
- Learn at least a little graphic design.
- Master the art of the giveaway.
- Post often (or as often as you can).
- Be consistent.
- Keep posting even if your only followers are friends and family.
- Find a mentor.
- Learn how to take power naps.

Scott became my knight in shining armor as he ran the machine that made my blog into a bona fide business. One of the first things he did after we started working together was find a way to take advantage of the amazing amount of traffic that the site was getting. At that point, my website had only Google ads, and even with just those few ads, the site was generating more income than I'd ever hoped for. Scott felt that I'd barely begun to scratch the surface, and he turned out to be correct. He took his considerable skills of persuasion and started opening doors to other ad networks. I always said that Scott could charm the fuzz off a peach. Although I had tried and been unsuccessful up to that point to contact the BlogHer network, with a few calls and e-mails, Scott managed to garner interest from a few different ad networks whose interest was more than piqued by the amount of traffic to the website, and they wanted "in." Within a few days of Scott's initial contact with BlogHer, we were on a conference call with the vice president, who is

With my business partner, Scott Warner, July 2012

good at her job. We signed a contract with BlogHer. They gave me their code, and their advertisers then displayed their ads on my blog.

Scott brought in a group of people who took a good hard look at what had become a "product" and were able to place a monetary value on my corporation. Subsequently, Scott bought into my company, and then I had not only a small corporation but also a business partner. Imagine my surprise when something so intangible that I started in the comfort of my living room late at night actually had a monetary value. I was amazed and satisfied, but honestly, I could not get over how innocently it had all begun. To say that it didn't bolster my ego and faith in my abilities would be false, but still, shock was the frontrunner in terms of my reaction. I thought about the time I had bartered with Britta's dance school—lessons for her and a website for them. I guess the seeds for this were in me all along, and now it was finally in full bloom with a harvest.

I got pretty lucky not just with the blog, but with Scott. Finding a partner who is incredibly smart, ambitious, and inventive, and whom I trust implicitly, is one of the best things that has happened in my life. Scott's business skills are invaluable, but I needed some hands-on assistance. I wasn't just Jill in that worn green chair anymore. Now, I was One Good Thing by Jillee, *Incorporated*. How crazy is that?

WORKING WITH FAMILY

I feel very fortunate to work with several members of my immediate and extended family, despite the fact that I am often told it's a bad idea. I personally think the pros far outweigh the cons, but I do acknowledge it has the potential to get messy.

Pros

- You get to work with people you like.
- You have familiarity with one another's quirks and strengths.
- There is instant camaraderie.
- Trust is already in place.

Cons

- It is harder to discipline a friend or family member.
- It is very hard to fire a friend or family member.
- If things go sour, family relationships can be ruined.

Okay, so maybe the pros don't *far* outweigh the cons, but I still think working with family can be a wonderful thing, as long as you adhere to a few ground rules:

Define Roles and Expectations

Don't assume anything. Instead, define your family member's job description as you would for any new employee and resist the urge to micromanage. Write out job responsibilities with as much detail as possible. This will help ensure that all business needs are covered and each member is happy with his or her assigned duties.

Resolve Conflicts

In order to get along, it's important to think before you react to something that your family member/employee has done to upset you. Be sure to share your feelings. Don't let a grudge fester and drive a wedge between family members. Talk it out and move forward.

Set Boundaries

Separating work from the personal is key. Keep business confined to work and handle personal stuff on your own time. Don't let the two overlap, or you will never get a break. Working with family can be really fun, but if you spend all day working with them and gossiping about life, when you go out for a family dinner, you probably won't have much left to say.

Be a Cheerleader

Encourage your family members. A quick compliment can go a long way, and likewise, a negative comment can have even more detrimental impact than you realize. By acknowledging each family member's strengths, each person feels individually valuable to the team and appreciated by the group as a whole.

Communicate

If the lines of communication are open, there's less potential for confusion and inaccurate assumptions. Talk to each other. Listen to each other's plans, ideas, and thoughts for the future. Again, make no assumptions. In this case, don't assume that family members know you well enough to understand when they've done something to irritate you. Talking about problems as they arise will help to correct the problem immediately and avoid more down the line. It will also minimize the potential for future resentment.

If you establish guidelines from the start, working with family members can be a very rewarding experience. I feel very fortunate to work with people who mean so much to me.

As the blog continued to grow as both a resource to a community of followers and as a revenue source for me, I realized that if I wanted to take this adventure to the next level (and even further from there), I was going to need some help beyond what Scott was able to provide. I needed day-to-day assistance. Right now, the blog averages seven million page views a month, with visitors checking in roughly a hundred thousand times a day. And with all those views, there are people writing comments. Imagine checking your inbox and seeing

Erik and Kaitlyn's engagement photo, 2011

that you have over a hundred e-mails and comments that need to be answered each day, in addition to writing a daily blog post and tending to your husband, kids, and home. I decided to make my little family corporation into an even bigger family business.

I hired my daughter-in-law, Kaitlyn (Erik's wife), who is now my full-time assistant and absolutely priceless. And she has a short commute to work, since she and Erik live in our basement apartment as Erik finishes college. I guess the idea of married kids who are just starting out and living with their parents until they're on their feet is now officially a family tradition! One of Kaitlyn's roles is to handle all of the e-mails that come in through the contact page and all of the comments posted directly on the blog. We have very powerful spam filters, but she makes certain that nothing inappropriate slips through, and then she runs everything by me. And there's a lot. She is my invaluable second set of eyes. She's also my personal travel agent and books all my appearances, and fields correspondence with prospective advertisers. She has even begun helping me with blog posts on occasion as my schedule gets busier. She does all of this . . . and she's also a great daughter-in-law!

Needless to say, I have learned to delegate. Entrepreneurs and small business owners often wear a lot of hats and tend to suffer from the "if I want something done right, I have to do it myself" mentality. However, trying to do it all yourself can be bad for business (not to mention your mental health). When I began my blog, I was a complete control freak. I was convinced that if I handled everything myself, it would get done faster and better. But over time, I realized that delegating to others is not only helpful but also crucial to your success. Delegating saves time and allows you to focus on the bigger and more important aspects of your work. Plus, giving your team members more responsibility sends the message that you have faith in them, you value their skills, and you are invested in seeing them grow and succeed in their own careers. If letting go isn't quite your strong suit, try these tips from a reformed control freak:

THE ART OF DELEGATING

Learn to Let Go

Take a deep breath and actively think about the fact that when you delegate something, it's now off of your plate. As hard as letting go may seem, wait until you see the final product before deciding whether or not you made the right decision.

Think of Time as an Investment

If you put thirty minutes into delegating a task instead of doing it yourself, then you gain that time back by teaching someone else an essential skill that will give you a return on your time investment down the road.

Focus on What You Love

Trying to manage every little aspect of your business hinders you from doing what you love the most. Focus on the most important aspects of your work and leave the minutiae to others.

Check In, but Don't Be Overbearing

Once you delegate a task, give your team members flexibility with how they get it done. Hovering over a project doesn't encourage anyone to succeed. But feel free to check in periodically to make sure everyone is on the right track and that they aren't needing guidance.

Remember That Different Isn't Wrong

Doing a task a certain way may work for you, but it doesn't mean that it's the only way to do it. Take the time to set the guidelines and goals of a project, then let your team carry out the task. Their approach might be different, and that's okay.

Acknowledge and Reward

It's important to show appreciation. Expressing appreciation communicates to your team that you value and care about the effort that they put in day in and day out. A simple "thank you" is often enough.

When we take the time and effort to delegate, the end result is that we can rely on the work of others and we will get better results than those we can achieve on our own.

Britta is my social media manager. She helps with my posts on Facebook, Twitter, Instagram, and Pinterest and develops strategies when it comes to both increasing traffic and managing the blog's exposure. And like Kaitlyn, she has also started contributing blog posts, for which I am extremely grateful. She's invaluable—and the best daughter anyone could ask for. I truly don't know what I would do without Britta. I would never have the time to spend navigating that vast new world of social media. I often marvel that kids of Britta's generation were born doing this sort of thing. I remember when my family got our first microwave and it was like something from outer space, but my kids intuitively knew how to heat up a pizza without reading the manual. She's 2G2BT because it's 511 for me going BT. (Translation: She's too good to be true because it's too much information for me going between technologies. LOL.) Erik is also involved. In between his studies, he

Britta and me at a blog conference, January 2014

tends to marketing One Good Thing. I'm wondering when Sten and Kell will hop on board.

SOCIAL MEDIA DOS AND DON'TS

Social media can be a great way to connect with people and has revolutionized interpersonal relations in all areas of our lives. While it may seem like uncharted territory with lots of potential pitfalls, in some situations, it can have as much value as talking to people in real-life situations. The same common sense and polite behavior applies. Here are a few dos and don'ts for navigating the social media landscape:

Don't Be Impulsive

When you feel urgently compelled to respond to a critical comment—wait. If you respond to a post that makes you defensive or angry, you will likely only make the situation worse. Consider waiting ten minutes, an hour, or even until the next day to respond. Bottom line is: Think before you press "send." The moment something is out there in cyberspace, you cannot take it back.

Don't Insult People

Hold this proverb dear: "If you don't have anything nice to say, don't say anything at all."

Do Learn When to Walk Away

Even when there is heated debate, discussion, or criticism about either you personally or your business, a continued back-and-forth dialogue often fuels the fire. If you don't engage, you'll be surprised how quickly the negative conversation dies down—and people leave you alone.

Do Check Your Grammar and Spelling

Common grammar errors stick out like sore thumbs, and unfortunately, people judge you by your appearance as well as your grammatical and spelling presence on the Internet. Make a habit of proofreading everything before you hit "send."

Don't Use Social Media to Vent

Status updates are not a forum for you to air your daily grievances. If you find yourself complaining all the time, stop. It doesn't matter whether or not your anger or grievance is justified. Rants will make you appear as a negative person who no one will want to be around—even virtually.

When in Doubt, Don't Say It

Because social media feels like a place where people can just be themselves and say things off the cuff, people often say things that they wouldn't typically say in public. Deleting tweets and updates doesn't solve the problem. If you don't want something coming back to you, don't say it online.

Don't Overshare

Don't flood your social media networks. People are interested in having a conversation with you, not just listening to you talk. Don't post a status update for every song you listen to. Caring is not oversharing.

Do Be Considerate When Tagging

Tagging photos of your friends and family with their names is a great way to share your photos, but not everyone wants pictures of themselves in a bathing suit splashed across the Internet.

Do Remember the Golden Rule

"Do unto others as you would have others do unto you." Be polite, and (hopefully) people will be polite in kind. You want people to leave insightful comments, so do the same for them. Be the example you'd like others to follow.

The bottom line is that although it sounds obvious, we need to always remember that social media sites are public. Even if you're extremely careful with your privacy settings, it's best to not post anything that you wouldn't want your grandmother or your boss to see.

I take to the green chair every once in a while when I need to come down to earth, but my working family and I never huddle and cuddle in it (even for old time's sake). But as the company grew, I came to realize the need for an office. In the beginning, it never even occurred to me to create an "official" office for myself. In fact, it took a sponsored blog post opportunity from Martha Stewart Home Office to get me even thinking about it. But as soon as a new office became a way to promote the blog—and also get a new office—I was all over it! I kicked two of the boys out of their room (seriously, one went to a room downstairs and one moved to the bedroom next to his . . . I'm not that heartless), painted my new office my favorite shade of sunny yellow, and bought a fun desk from Ikea, an armchair from a consignment shop, a few bookshelves, and a nice *big* monitor. I was in heaven. I no longer had to strain my eyes to see the photos that I was trying to edit on my thirteen-inch laptop screen, and I had an entire closet for files and supplies. Perhaps most importantly, I had a door, and I could close it if I needed to. The truth is, I rarely close it, because I still work best when

I'm connected to the hustle and bustle of everyday home life. But just knowing that I have the option of closing the door is good enough for me.

So, now we all work from home in a newly designed office. Kaitlyn works at her computer in the basement, but she emerges every so often, and Britta works from her apartment, but pops in and out during the day. Our business is homespun and really cozy. Once a week, we all drive to Scott's office in Provo for a business meeting, which is not unlike the kind of meeting one has at a television station or newspaper where everyone puts their heads together and maps out what the day or week will look like. Two heads are better than one, and five are really superior, but all of it starts and ends with me and my fingers to the keyboard.

Last but not least, there's Dave. His current title is chief cheerleader, and he leads the squad that consists of Kell and Sten. Dave is awesome, even though he has an intense day job as director of photography for the Church of Jesus Christ of Latter-day Saints, which takes him all over the world.

The only problem with my business is that I have an extremely demanding boss. She doesn't seem to realize that I still have domestic responsibilities like laundry, grocery shopping, and cooking. I also have PTA meetings, school orientation days, driving the younger kids here and there, and all that stuff that we moms do invisibly as we facilitate our children's lives. And what about tending to myself? You know, like taking a manicure and pedicure break? Does my boss ever stop to think about that? I blog until the wee hours and I'm awake by six-thirty in the morning to make breakfast and see the kids off to school and Dave off to work. And sometimes my boss gets a little irritable when I'm writing or answering e-mails and Dave plops himself

Dave at work

down in the extra chair in my office because he wants to chat, and I try

not to say, "Hey! Just because I work from home doesn't mean I'm not

at work!" But I don't say that, despite the boss's frown, because the truth

is that I am so grateful that he can just pop in and we can have our

fifteen minutes of conversation that we promised to have every day. But

that boss of mine disapproves of socializing at work. I try to ignore her.

Doesn't she realize that working from home isn't nine to five, but more

like 24/7, and all employees need a break?

It makes me laugh when I think about how hard I thought it was working for someone else now that I work for me. Since I am such a tough employer, I have learned some tricks to motivate and discipline myself when working at home so I don't get in trouble with the boss!

TIPS FOR BEING DISCIPLINED AND PRODUCTIVE WHEN YOU WORK FROM HOME

Get Organized

Decide which portion of your house will be called your home office and then organize it. Even if all you need to work is a laptop, make sure that you have a desk for yourself that is separate from the hustle and bustle of your home.

Plan Your Day

If you don't know what you need to do, or what's coming up, it can be difficult to be productive. So plan your day as completely as you can, the same way as you would if you worked in a traditional office atmosphere. This could be as simple as creating a quick list each morning. Some things may change, but this will at least set your expectations for what you need to achieve.

Take Breaks

Just as in any job, breaks are important. When I am sitting at my desk, typing on my computer, I completely lose track of time. It's helpful for me to actually set an alarm on my phone that will alert me when it's time to take a break. Often that "break" involves starting dinner preparation or throwing in a load of laundry, but, for me, that is part of the beauty of working at home.

Avoid Home Distractions

The fridge, the TV, endless household chores, and even family members are just a few other distractions you encounter when working at home. Having a separate office space can help minimize distractions, but ultimately it is up to you to stay focused.

Leave Your Pajamas in the Bedroom

As I've already admitted, this one is hard for me. You don't necessarily have to wear office attire, but getting up, taking a shower, and dressing for the day will help to keep you in a mind-set that you are working rather than relaxing at home. You'll also avoid the embarrassment of having the UPS driver catch you in your pajamas at two o'clock in the afternoon. (Not that I would know anything about that.)

Know When to Stop

This may be the hardest thing of all for me. I tend to do a lot of my writing and catching up on e-mails late at night, because that's when distractions are at a minimum. One of the best things about working from home for me is not punching a time clock. But anyone who works from home needs to know when enough is enough. I know that this is easier said than done, but when you have reached your goals for the day, turn off the computer and walk away.

WHENEVER I TRAVEL to blogging conventions or speak to groups, the question I am most frequently asked is, "Can you really make any money just blogging?" I just smile and say yes, lots of companies like to advertise their products on blogs because bloggers have very loyal followers. The power of the blogosphere has been quite an eye-opening experience for me. My journey from neophyte blogger to savvy businesswoman is still just beginning. Every day I learn more about how this crazy new world works and how much bloggers, in general, are underutilized, underpaid, and generally underestimated. I aim to make a difference in that arena—and yet, at my very essence, I'm still a wife and mother first. Success has not spoiled Jillee—and that is one good thing for sure.

TIPS FOR BALANCING: ACHIEVING YOUR DREAMS WHILE TENDING TO YOUR FAMILY

Balancing the requirements of work and family can be challenging, to say the least, and I don't know if there is such a thing as the perfect balance. There is surely no such thing as being able to do it all. But it is possible to find an acceptable balance between profession and parenthood. The key is to focus on a plan, get organized, and realize that sometimes imbalance is inevitable and you just have to accept that.

Let Go of Guilt

Rather than dwell on not being with your child as much as you might want to be, think about how greatly your career benefits your family.

At conferences in D.C. and
Salt Lake City, 2014

Come to terms with your choices and focus on the priorities. Accept that
there will be good and bad days.

Guilt is one of the greatest wastes of emotional energy. It can im-
mobilize us. Guilt is debilitating. By introducing logic to help counter-
balance the guilt, you can avoid sabotaging your efforts toward work/
family balance and stay on course better.

Limit Distractions and Time-Wasters

At home, be disciplined and set time limits when checking e-mail or making phone calls. At your workplace, try to avoid distractions that will make you less productive. The more time spent procrastinating and wasting time, the less time spent with family or on yourself.

Learn to Say No

Practice the ability to put work down and say no to additional responsibilities for which you don't have time. Let go of workplace worries while away from the office.

Keep One Calendar

Putting personal and professional items on the same calendar prevents meetings and appointments from overlapping with family commitments. Make sure every day's details are accounted for as well—laundry, meal-planning, after-school activities, meetings with clients, doctor's appointments . . . you get the picture.

Organize and Delegate

Improving your delegation and time-management skills can buy time needed for your family and yourself. Set priorities. Work smarter, not harder . . . and really let go! Create lists and save them for reuse.

Build a Support Network

Recruit friends, family, neighbors, bosses, work colleagues, and whomever else might be of assistance to you and ask for their support. Between work and family, it's often easy to get thrown off course. Be prepared by creating backup and emergency plans.

Enjoy Quality Time with Your Family

Making time for your kids is crucial to nurture your family relationships. Give them your full attention. Develop rituals you can all look forward to. It doesn't really matter what you do as long as you do it together.

Spend Time with Your Partner

Remember to nurture your relationship with your partner. Often, if you're busy with work and home, your partner is the first to get neglected. Discover activities you can do together—whether it is hiking, dancing, or taking cooking classes, as long as you are together, you are providing the relationship with nourishment to grow and flourish.

Create Moments for Yourself

If everything is going out and nothing is coming back in, pretty soon you'll be running on empty. Take time to care for yourself. Take a bath, read a novel, go for a walk, listen to music. Eat a healthy diet, include physical activity in your daily routine, and get enough sleep.

Hopefully these tips will help you find an acceptable work-home balance. Beware, however, that just when you think you've found a nice balance, life has a way of tipping the scales. When this happens, remember to take a deep breath (or a few) until you can get back on an even keel.

People also ask to what I attribute the phenomenal growth of my blog. I usually say it was just the right message at the right time. A message about being frugal and being a wise steward of resources. What I have come to realize is that as I acknowledged and blogged about one good thing each day, I was, subconsciously, taking one step at a time as I got myself back on my feet to my new normal. For sure, my recent history helped fuel the growth of the blog, because people appreciate people who are "real" and have the courage to tell people that they aren't perfect. I don't want to hide who I was or what I have been through. I could have omitted the part of my journey through rehab, but I don't, and frankly, it never even occurred to me to do so.

From the very beginning, I wrote honestly in the website's suggested "About Me" page. There is a photo of me above one line that says, *California girl, transplanted and blooming in Utah. In recovery and loving life!* The two words *in recovery* are highlighted and link back to the story of my battle with addiction. I put it out there so that anyone who is fighting a similar battle or is simply curious about addictions could find out more. My purpose was to share my experience and give strength and hope to those readers who struggle in their own lives— and not just those with addiction. The responses to my journey continue to run the entire spectrum of human emotion and come primarily from those who battle addiction: from the pure joy of someone who has also overcome addiction and is buoyed by a kindred spirit, to the somber confessions of people who state that they need to seek help, to those who are still deeply into their addiction. Honestly, sometimes the comments are tough to read and make me cry—for those who are healed and those who are still suffering.

Although I didn't know it consciously at the time, the omission of "About Me" would have obstructed my continued healing. I no longer felt ashamed of my journey as I had in the past. I was moving forward. I also wanted people to know that we all have our struggles and crosses to bear. Being connected to one another is a powerful force for good in the world.

twelve

Once Upon a Then and Now

S ometimes I wonder what would happen if I could change my journey thus far. I wonder what life would be like if I had never taken
that first drink that sent me on a path I never anticipated in my wildest
nightmares. My knee-jerk reaction is that had I known then what I
know now, I never would have even tried a sip of alcohol. But then I
think, maybe I wouldn't be where I am today if *not* for this journey.
Maybe the perilous detour was simply my destiny as I departed from
what began as a seemingly idyllic life. I'll never know the answer. I
have to believe that my journey has brought me to not only a good
place, but perhaps an even better place.

The cold hard truth is that I am still in recovery. You don't go to
rehab and then live happily ever after. Life is not a fairy tale. Recovery
is a permanent state of being, and the entire burden of control and responsibility is entirely up to me. Sometimes it's pretty brutal and scary.
I have no one but myself to rely on in this respect. I can't expect family
or friends to be my watchdogs or bodyguards. That would be unfair.

Maintaining the state of recovery is most challenging when I am on the road—traveling to blog conventions, vacationing with my family, going to speaking engagements. That's when the seductive power of alcohol beckons like a siren, and it takes everything in my power not to succumb to its call. Temptation tantalizes me at the airport as travelers sit in the airport bars sipping wine, Bloody Marys, and icy beers. It lurks in the hotel lobby bars as people toast one another's arrivals in a new city. It prowls around at parties and receptions, where cocktails and champagne are the drinks of choice for celebrations and festivities.

There are triggers everywhere, and I can't take a chance of slipping up because, for me, there is no such thing as "just one drink." I have to accept that social drinking is not a possibility. To this day, if I am at dinner with someone who leaves a half glass of wine untouched, I can't process why or how they didn't finish their glass. Not only is alcohol an addiction for me, it is an obsession. As you know, I've had slips since the Ark released me, and they scared the living daylights out of me. I know where the mistake can take me—and although the Ark served me well, I never want to be a resident there again. Sometimes the process of constantly exercising self-control makes me want to cry and scream. I hate the battle between me and the bottle. But I have to face the fact that I am an addict and I cannot take recovery—which is far too fragile a status—for granted.

BREAKING BAD HABITS

I am all too often faced with situations that encourage drinking. Throw in the fact that many business trips usually have an element of stress and anxiety attached to them, and the temptation can be a slippery slope for someone like me. For the longest time I simply told myself I just had to be strong, that this was just the way things were and I had to cope. But with the help of some good advice from a good friend, I have come to realize all these triggers can be managed if I know how to identify them and deal with them.

Memory plays a powerful role in each person's life and can ignite a unique emotional trigger that can lead to the indulgence of an impulse. For example, hearing a particular song may remind you of a love affair gone wrong; seeing a couple pushing a baby stroller may trigger sadness over the baby you lost or so desperately want; gossiping with coworkers could bring back painful images of high school cliques. It is important to identify your own triggers so that you can deal with them in a constructive way.

A Few Exercises to Help Control Unwelcome Impulses

Return to the Present

Triggers are often products of some past event. Remember that the situation you are thinking of is not happening now; it already occurred and you need to remain focused on the present. Relax and breathe.

Do What You Can to Heal the Situation

The only way to move on and fully let go is to empower yourself to do so. If you are having difficulty making progress on your own, professional help can make a big difference.

Explore Alternatives

Brainstorm new strategies that you can use when your triggers are firing. List some productive and enjoyable activities that you can substitute for negative actions.

Find the Blessings in Disguise

For example, instead of being angry at your ex-boyfriend who cheated on you, thank your lucky stars you are out of that relationship.

I might have gone on drinking the way that I did if not for the fact that I hit rock bottom on that auspicious and symbolic Thanksgiving Day. It has become even more of a day of gratitude for me, encompassing far more significance than ever before. Perhaps if I hadn't ended up on the couch in the lobby of that hotel with a stranger's coat covering my shoulders, I might never have had the wake-up call that I so desperately needed and tried to deny. Had I kept on that destructive path, alcohol might have chipped away at my heart and soul, causing irreparable damage. My drinking might have destroyed my family. It might have caused me to take the life of someone else as I fooled myself into thinking that I was safe to drive a car. It makes me shudder to consider the possibilities. When I go to AA meetings, I see people who are fooling themselves (or trying to) as they walk the walk to satisfy the demands of a family or fulfill a community service requirement for a DUI, and they pain me because I know they are suffering. My family cared enough about me and loved me so unconditionally that they intervened, but deep down inside I must have wanted to save myself. When it comes to addiction of any kind, no one but you can truly save you.

When I saw the young people in the Ark, kids not much older than my own children, I wondered what pain their parents went through as their children battled addictions. I thought of my own children and sighed a breath of relief that I haven't known that pain firsthand as a parent. I thought about my parents and the torment they suffered as they saw me fall down the rabbit hole. I now realize how tough it was for my father to go from calling his little girl "Jilly Bean" to calling her a "drunk." As we get older, the years between us and our parents close. We gain perspective and view them not only as mom and dad, but as man and woman and husband and wife, too. We develop a greater understanding and appreciation. In my case, that appreciation is now outsize after the unconditional love that my parents showed me even during my darkest hours, which I realize now were probably some of their darkest hours as well.

THE FIFTEEN MOST IMPORTANT LESSONS MY PARENTS TAUGHT ME

No book about my life would be complete without a section devoted solely to my parents, who I happen to think are the most wonderful parents in the entire universe. I don't say that lightly, because I know there are many, many people who don't enjoy the same feelings and relationship with their parents. I am very blessed in this area of my life. They are both amazing role models and continue to inspire me as I try to pattern my life after theirs. I have been the recipient of their pure, unconditional love and acceptance—which made all the difference during some of my darkest hours.

I sincerely wish I could share my parents' gifts with the whole world. It is the gift of knowing that no matter how far you fall from grace, those whom you love and who love you will stick by you through it all. Since I don't have the power to grant that wish, allow me to share some of the things I have learned from my parents that have made my life rich and sweet.

My parents, February 2014

Forgiveness. Life is too short to spend it being vengeful or bitter. My parents taught me that however hard it feels, forgiveness is imperative: to free ourselves from the pain and darkness we carry when we have hurt someone or hurt ourselves.

Work Ethic. My father is a self-made man who achieved great success in business without a college degree. My mother attained her college degree and then raised six children while married to a man who worked long hours. They also devoted many hours to volunteer church work each week. Their example taught me that hard work is its own reward.

Service. My parents are strong believers in the motto "Where much is given, much is required." We were given opportunities to do service often, with our parents right there by our sides, leading by example. They set an example that began when we were small and continued throughout our lives that life is about giving, not receiving.

Consistency. My parents were consistent in both their discipline and their love. Knowing where my parents stood on the important things in life was a great comfort to me as a child.

Independence. My fiercely independent streak largely results from the fact that my parents encouraged me to try new things with a sense of adventure. Looking back, particularly as a parent myself now, I'm sure it was hard on my parents when I went to New York City for a summer internship after I graduated from college. But they never made me doubt my decision or hinted at their own angst. When I first moved to North Dakota for my first job, I cried on the phone to them for hours because I was homesick. They listened, but never suggested I pack my bags and come home.

Acceptance. Despite the fact that my parents both come from small towns and very traditional upbringings, they have always been accepting and inclusive of everyone with whom they meet and interact. There was never even a whisper of prejudice or judgment. Not to mention that even as faithful LDS church members, they accepted and helped me through my addiction.

Thrift. My parents were products of the Great Depression, and even though they achieved financial success over the years, they never forgot their roots and taught me to be a wise steward of resources.

Adventure. The summer that my youngest sister turned eight, my parents flew us to San Francisco for dinner. One summer when I was about sixteen, we explored parts of Canada in an RV.

When I was in my teens, my older sister and I accompanied my parents on trips to Spain, England, and Morocco. My parents traveled to many other places on their own as well. They instilled a desire in me to see the world. There was always another adventure waiting around the corner that kept us on our toes and made life exciting and sweet. It is important to note that adventure can also take place in your own backyard. Consider a tent and campfire, complete with s'mores and ghost stories!

Generosity. Every Christmas Eve for as long as I can remember, my parents would load all the kids into the station wagon for a late-night Secret Santa run to the home of a family less fortunate than ours. We'd "doorbell ditch" the house, leaving the box that my mom filled with presents, food, and an envelope of cash. It was great fun and a tradition I carry on in my own family today. Giving your time and resources to others less fortunate is something we all need to learn and teach.

Open Hearts. My mother has been known to invite strangers to dinner. There was always room for one more at our Thanksgiving table. One day, my mom went out of her way to be kind to a foul-tempered lady who worked at the post office, and made a lifelong friend.

Spirituality. My parents have strong, unshakable faith that has pulled our family through many trials and provided a lifetime of peace and blessings. Worship has always been important to us. Then and now.

Self-esteem. My mother always told me I could do anything I wanted to do and be anything I wanted to be. She said that my gifts and abilities were unique. Now that I am a mother myself, I try to do the same for my kids and hope that they believe me as I believed my mom and subsequently believe in themselves.

The Importance of the Arts. My siblings and I were all given opportunities to take piano, dance, and singing lessons. We often attended theater—both plays and musicals—and even the occasional opera and ballet.

Tradition. The Flour Game, the Birthday Treasure Hunt, strawberry waffles on Thanksgiving and Christmas morning, Secret Santa, Easter sunrise service, family talent shows . . . I could go on and on. These traditions reinforced our values and beliefs and provided us with colorful family memories.

Good Food. My mom is a *wonderful* cook. With a few rare exceptions, I always loved everything she made. She took pride in cooking and baking for her family and loved listening to cooking shows on the radio.

I cannot thank my parents enough for all their good lessons, which taught me how to find fulfillment. Despite the pain and challenges I've endured, and how far my life veered off course, I believe that the knowledge and tools instilled in me by my parents truly saved me.

It is important for people to understand that addiction to alcohol is not a moral issue or misconduct. It is a disease recognized by medical professionals. I suppose that's true, and who am I to question scientific authorities, but for me, there remains an aspect of being drunk that defied every one of my principles—morally, religiously, and personally as a daughter, wife, and mother. Under the influence, I was blind to the deleterious effects as I justified my drinking and rationalized my ability to be in control.

Each morning when I awakened semi-sober and yet hungover, my insolence riddled me with guilt, and yet the only panacea was to have yet another drink. I felt bad about myself for drinking, and as I was caught in the vortex of addiction, the worse I felt, the more I drank, and the more I drank, the worse I felt. The vicious cycle was nearly impossible to break. It did not feel like an illness, perhaps because that felt like an easy excuse. Placing blame on something other than myself— even medical fact—might have obstructed my path to recovery. I had to take full responsibility. I accept the truth that I must still and always remain vigilant. I must concede that the desire for alcohol will never go away. I remind myself constantly that alcohol affects me most adversely: It affects me quickly and it causes me to be anxious. Many people use alcohol to quell anxiety. I am not like those people. Yes, I envy people who can be social drinkers, but I have to make peace with the fact that I am not one of them. Indeed, hindsight is twenty-twenty. I can't go back and change things that have happened in my life, but I can weave each new day in the spirit of a beautiful embroidery yet to be completed and move forward as who I am now and who I want to continue to be.

I OFTEN LAUGH when people say, "Don't you wish that you could be twenty-five again?" Sure! What would be wrong with having not one wrinkle, not a sag anywhere, a thicker head of hair, and skin the color of toast as I basked in the California sun before anyone knew its hazard?

I am struck by the fearlessness of youth. What was I thinking—or not thinking—when I moved from the comfort of my parents' home in sunny California to the frozen tundra of Bismarck? How did I muster the gumption to stand in front of the camera and report the news, weather, and—for goodness' sake—sports? How did I pack up and move to Minnesota without a job on the horizon, and then back to California, and then out to Utah with little kids and a husband who was commuting across three states to another job? How was I not exhausted as I searched and searched for more and more?

But here's the thing: I would want to be twenty-five again only if I knew then what I know now. Now, that would be perfection! At fifty-two, I feel at peace. I embrace loving life and being comfortable in my own skin (even if the "own skin" part is helped along with various store-bought and homemade magic potions that promise to at least temporarily regain that youthful glow).

Kidding aside, probably the single most rewarding aspect of being over fifty is no longer being concerned with what people think of me. That was so important when I was a teenager and a young wife and mother as I battled so many self-esteem issues. Despite my parents' love and support when I was a child and my husband's love, no one can be a dream weaver for you regardless of how hard they try. Of course, I want people to like me, but I have the confidence now to live my life for myself and my family. I am neither concerned about being judged nor do I judge others. My life, as fraught as it can be professionally, is simpler now as I hold dear to a less complicated philosophy: Lift others up, do your best to rescue those who are less fortunate, and basically do unto others as you would have them do unto you. This is not only the mantra for me, but the one that is the basis for my blog. At fifty-two, even on days that feel endless and when a close look in the mirror makes me jump back because the woman I see is a little older than the one I was expecting, I feel sane.

I shake my head as I realize what is not just sane but also ridiculously obvious: Home is where the heart is and life is really the best that it can be if you just focus on one good thing on a daily basis. But it takes the abandon of youth and all that energy as you run down the road at breakneck speed to realize that you can stop and find yourself with everything at your fingertips, because it was really there all along.

In the years since I left the Ark, I have focused on feathering my nest. I have my office, and slowly but surely we are redoing the kitchen—refacing cabinets and just sprucing things up. I realized when I left the Ark that keeping house and keeping Jill go hand in hand. We both needed to be renewed and brought into the light. The only remnant from the past is that worn green chair. I might relocate her to the basement when I decide to make a playroom for future grandchildren, but I'll never let her go. There's a beauty in her venerable spirit. I hope to age the way in which she has. I want to sit in her arms as I tell stories with grandkids on my lap. We all have stories to tell: stories that make us laugh and stories about hard times with endings that make us cry or happily surprise us. Don't think for one second that I feel my story of struggle is tougher than someone else's. I am fully aware that I am one of the lucky ones.

No one's life is a fairy tale, but there has been something of a magical aspect to mine, and I feel blessed.

Once upon a time there was a girl named Jill who wanted to write and wanted her life to be perfect in what she didn't realize was an imperfect world. She wasn't exactly sure what her stories would be about, but she wanted to reach as many people as she could and have her name in lights. She met a handsome boy named Dave who wanted to chase storms with his camera and never settle down in one place for too long. Then something funny happened: The ambitious girl who reached for the stars and the adventurous boy who chased storms fell in love, married, and had four children.

The girl became a wife and mother, and the boy became a videographer, husband, and father, and both of them let go of dreams that were now reduced to fantasy. Of course, they loved each other and their children, but something was missing from their lives, although they paid little attention to the void as they moved on and cared for their family.

In the girl's search for something more, she stumbled and fell. Her injuries were severe, but the boy and their children banded together and rescued her, even though she went kicking and screaming at first, refusing to believe that she needed anyone's help. Now, all fairy tales have some hidden meaning, and here it's definitely that love conquers all—but you have to believe.

Once the girl believed, she returned home to heal. As time went on, she felt safe within the confines of her family's love, and rediscovered the nearly lost love she held for herself. She remembered that passion from her early years and started to write the way she once promised herself she would a long time ago. Lo and behold, her name went up in lights! The boy recalled his sense of adventure, took out his camera, and chased those storms—some caused by weather and some man-made—and traveled the world. Their children continued to grow with beauty, courage, and wisdom from life lessons in both hard ways and good ways.

At the end of each day, the girl writes one good thing and shares it with a lot of people—most of whom are strangers, but she feels that they are friends.

And the girl is determined that she and her family will live happily ever after.

thirteen

One Good Thing by Jillee's Greatest Hits

*mom's amazing
sour cream cookies*

Every year around Christmastime I get requests from friends and neighbors for my recipe for "those delicious soft sugar cookies." I have probably made thousands of them over the years for special occasions and as Christmas gifts for neighbors and co-workers. It is one of those recipes that never fails to delight.

In our family they are called sour cream cookies, although the name hardly does them justice. Think Granny B's or Lofthouse Cookies, but way better! Not only are they so thick and soft, but they're also coated with a thick layer of yummy powdered sugar frosting.

While they aren't hard to make, there are some definite tried-and-true tips that make them turn out perfect. If you're a fan of big, soft, frosted sugar cookies, this recipe is for you. I usually double this recipe when I'm making cookies for gifts. A single recipe will make approximately 24 big cookies.

If you make these and give them away at Christmas—or any other time—don't be surprised if the recipients come knocking on your door wanting the recipe.

3 cups all-purpose flour

2 tsp baking powder

1 tsp baking soda

1 tsp salt

½ cup shortening (*not* butter)

1 cup sugar

2 large eggs

1 cup sour cream

1 tsp vanilla extract

In a medium bowl, combine the flour, baking powder, baking soda, and salt.

In the bowl of an electric mixer fitted with a paddle attachment (or use a hand mixer), beat the shortening and sugar together on medium-high speed until soft and fluffy. Beat in the eggs one at a time, mixing well after each addition. Add the sour cream and vanilla extract and blend together until creamy.

With the mixer on low speed, add the dry ingredients (I add a third of the mixture at a time), mixing just until incorporated and evenly mixed.

You will have very sticky dough at this point, so it is very important to *chill the dough for 1 to 2 hours.* The waiting is the hardest part!

After the dough has chilled, the rest of the process is about technique. Here are some tips to make sure that your cookies come out just like my mom's.

Preheat the oven to 350 degrees.

Divide the dough into two portions so you can roll out one section at a time. It's easier to work with smaller pieces.

With plenty of flour on your board to avoid sticking issues, roll out the dough, aiming for a thickness of approximately ¼ inch. Don't work the dough too much or it will get tough. Make sure to flour your rolling pin and cookie cutters as well.

Cut out your cookies, scoop them off the board with a spatula, and transfer them to a cookie sheet. It helps if you nudge a little bit of flour under the cookie dough as you lift it off the board.

Bake the cookies for 10 to 12 minutes. Timing is crucial, so keep an eye on them. You are shooting for cookies that are just *barely* starting to brown on the edges.

Allow the cookies to cool completely before putting on your favorite frosting. I'm adding my favorite frosting recipe on the next page because it's easy and yummy. I like to spread it generously on the cookie and top it off with sprinkles.

powdered sugar frosting

(I mostly eyeball these amounts.)

2 cups powdered sugar

2 tbsp softened butter

1 tsp vanilla

2 to 3 tbsp milk

Food coloring (I use a tiny dab of Wilton pink gel coloring.)

In a small bowl, mix sugar, butter, vanilla, food coloring, and 2 table-spoons of the milk. Keep adding milk about a teaspoon at a time until the frosting reaches the right consistency: not too thick, but not too runny.

Now go pour yourself a tall glass of ice-cold milk and enjoy the fruits of your labor. No doubt these aren't the easiest cookies to make, but they are oh-so-worth the effort! I hope you will agree.

my mom's wonderful english muffin bread

You can use regular yeast in this recipe, but then you'll have to let the dough rise twice: once in the bowl, till the dough reaches the top, and then in the pans, again till it reaches the top. With the rapid-rise yeast the dough need rise only once, in the pans.

5½ cups warm water

3¼ oz. packets rapid-rise yeast

2 tbsp salt

3 tbsp sugar

11 cups flour (I use bread flour, but my mom always used all-purpose.)

Butter

Preheat the oven to 350 degrees.

In a bowl, mix all the ingredients except the butter. Mix only enough to combine. The dough will be very sticky.

Spoon equal amounts of the dough into four loaf pans. (If using regular yeast, make sure to follow the instructions above.)

Let the dough rise until it reaches the top of the pans. Bake in a 350-degree oven for 45 minutes or until the loaves are a nice golden brown on all sides. Brush melted butter on top.

Let the loaves cool on cooling rack completely before attempting to slice—otherwise you will just have a mess on your hands. After the bread is done cooling, it slices up beautifully.

It is served best toasted. My very favorite way to eat En-

glish muffin bread is with butter and *honey.* Throw in a cup of hot chocolate and you will be in *heaven!*

And that's it. Easy, economical, and truly some of the most delicious toasting bread you will ever eat.

no-grate homemade liquid laundry detergent

Of all the homemade laundry products I have tried (and there have been many), this is the easiest to make, and it works every bit as well as the others. Recipe amounts here are for 1 gallon. I make 3 gallons at a time, lining up three 1-gallon jugs (old Minute Maid orange juice containers) and adding the ingredients in assembly-line style. I use a small plastic funnel for this; it helps make the process go much faster, with fewer spills.

3 tbsp borax
3 tbsp washing soda
2 tbsp Dawn Ultra dishwashing liquid
4 cups hot water
Cold water

Place the first three ingredients in a gallon container.

Pour the hot water into the container until all the ingredients are dissolved in the liquid. Fill the container almost to the top with cold water. (Bubbles will overflow out of the bottle a little.)

It is not a thick liquid detergent. It's quite thin, in fact. But it works just as well. It has few to no suds (just like grated-soap detergent), and it is fine to use in HE (high-efficiency) washers for that reason. Because it is thin, I end up using more of it—usually around ½ to 1 cup, more or less. But I am fine with that because it is so inexpensive (and easy) to make.

make a year's worth of powdered laundry detergent for $30!

A reader shared her version of homemade laundry detergent and claimed it lasted her family a year. A year's worth of laundry soap! That's an idea that is hard not to get behind. Since I'd been curious about making a powdered version of homemade laundry detergent, I decided to give it a try.

3 bars Fels-Naptha, grated ($1.33 for 3 bars)

1 76-oz box borax ($5.85)

1 55-oz box washing soda ($4.07)

2 cups baking soda ($0.53)

2 3-pound containers oxygen bleach, e.g., OxiClean (Sun brand at
the Dollar Store, $4.00 each)

1 to 2 28-oz containers Purex fabric softener crystals
(optional, $6.97)

To grate the bars of soap, I use my Blendtec, but you can also use a food processor. I added a cup of the oxygen bleach to each bar when I processed it. It seemed to help the blades do their job better.

Once you add everything, you have a lot of ingredients to mix together. I put it all in a kitchen garbage bag (doubled) and tumble it all together. Just tie it off tight and turn it over a handful of times and you're good to go. Use 2 tablespoons per load.

Note: Now you have a nicely integrated batch of laundry detergent that should last a family of four for one year. Since the Nystuls are over the "family of four" limit (my daughter still brings her laundry home to wash), this doesn't last us a full year, but it does last us a good four to six months.

· homemade stain remover ·

I was inspired to make this recipe after my eighteen-year-old, Kell, presented me with a shirt that had a big chocolate stain on the front of it. As if that weren't bad enough, it had apparently been sitting in the bottom of his dirty-clothes basket for a while. (I don't think I even want to know what *his* version of "a while" is.) For sure, this was the perfect opportunity to see how my homemade Shout performed under pressure.

⅔ cup Dawn dishwashing liquid

⅔ cup ammonia

6 tbsp baking soda

2 cups warm water

Mix everything together and pour into a spray bottle. (I got mine at Walmart for about a dollar.)

This mixture does tend to separate, but after a quick shake it's good to go.

To use: Spray on stains as you normally would. I usually let mine soak in for a few minutes at least. Then launder as usual.

Note: Since my particular chocolate stain posed a bit of an extra challenge, I took a few extra seconds (literally, that's all it took) to rub the fabric together where I'd sprayed. When I was finished, I was somewhat shocked to see the stain was practically already gone! (My old bottle of real Shout never did that.)

I tossed the shirt in the washer with some of my home-made laundry soap, and it came out clean and pristine. Even my son was impressed. I really don't think he believed I could prevail with this one. That'll teach him to doubt my laundering prowess.

I hope you find this helpful with your laundry room battles.

miracle laundry whitening solution

I'm one of those strange people who actually like doing laundry. And one of the things I like *most* about it is the sense of accomplishment I feel when something dirty comes out *clean*. I like the challenge aspect of it as well.

So when I came across this recipe for whitening whites in the comments section of my blog, I knew I had to try it. And I had the perfect test subject: a dingy mattress pad that I had washed time and time again, but that remained dingy and never seemed to return to its original white. But I *knew* there was a whiteness lurking under the dinginess. I just needed the right formula to apply to it. This one looked very promising.

Hot hot hot water
1 cup laundry detergent
1 cup powdered dishwasher detergent
1 cup bleach
½ cup borax

Fill the washing machine with hot water. (After I did so, I also dumped in a large pot of water I had brought to a boil on the stove. I was aiming for *hot hot hot* water.) Add the rest of the ingredients and the article you are trying to whiten. Keep the load size as small as possible. You are looking for concentrated cleaning power, and the more water you have in the tub, the less concentrated it will be. Shoot for *barely* enough water to cover the article.

Let soak for as long as you can stand it. I managed to stay away from it for a couple of hours. Overnight would work, too, and is probably best, if you can swing it. The whitening solution actually made a *big* difference on my mattress pad and released the white that was lurking within.

how to wash and whiten yellowed pillows

At first I hesitated doing this post because it teeters precariously on "too much information," but the more research I did, and the more I asked around, I realized that, over time, yellowing pillows are a pretty common thing.

One of the most common reasons pillows can turn yellow is sweat. Even when you're sleeping your body continues to perspire to keep itself at a comfortable temperature. Depending on the pillowcase fabric, perspiration can seep through. As the perspiration dries, it can leave a yellow stain on the pillow. Even if you use pillow protector covers underneath your pillowcases, the yellowing can still occur.

In the past when the yellowing got really bad, I would simply toss the pillow and buy a new one. But I hated doing that because the pillow was still perfectly good. Recently I came across an old article from *Martha Stewart Living* that suggested pillows should be washed at least twice a year. Wow. I hope I'm not the *only* one who didn't know that! I have washed an occasional pillow in the past, but usually because something had spilled on it.

After reading Martha's suggestion, I set out on a mission to systematically wash all of the pillows in the house, and since I was going to the trouble, I decided to address the yellowing issue at the same time and give them the Miracle Laundry Whitening Solution treatment.

Not only did the whole pillow-washing process turn out to be much easier than I anticipated, it worked like a charm.

Check the care label to confirm that your pillows (down or synthetic) are machine washable—most are. Be sure to remove the pillowcases and any pillow protectors.

Fill the washing machine about a third full with *hot* water. (I even added a couple of pots full of boiling water.)

Add all the ingredients in the Miracle Laundry Whitening Solution (or, if you're just looking to wash your pillows, add your detergent now), then start the machine and allow it to agitate for a few minutes to make sure all the detergent dissolves before you add the pillows.

Once the detergent is dissolved, add the pillows, and then allow the washer to fill the rest of the way with *hot* water. I washed two pillows at a time, which helped balance the load when it came time for the spin cycle.

Agitate the pillows for several minutes, then stop the machine, turn the pillows *over* to allow the top side to get the full effect of agitating in the hot water, then restart the machine and agitate for several minutes more.

Put your machine on the second rinse cycle or just run it through twice manually.

DRYING THE PILLOWS

For down- and feather-filled pillows, use the air cycle. For synthetics, use the low heat setting.

Place the pillow(s) in the dryer, and add a couple of tennis balls (tucked into a pair of clean socks) or a few homemade dryer balls to help fluff the pillows as they tumble dry. If it's a nice day you could also set them outside in the sun to dry.

GOOD-BYE TO YELLOW UNDERARM STAINS!

One day, the undershirts and T-shirts that my boys wore just bugged me to no end. Although all were relatively new, after a few wears, particularly after playing sports or whatever it is that boys do to get all sweaty and disgusting, the underarm areas were all stained yellow.

I tried everything I could possibly think of to get them white again. When I saw an article in *Glamour* magazine titled "The Only Spot Remover You Will Ever Need," I was intrigued. The mixture consisted of one part Dawn dishwashing liquid mixed with two parts hydrogen peroxide.

I knew the stains on my boys' T-shirts were über-stubborn (since even pouring straight bleach on them hadn't worked previously), so I used the above recipe plus some baking soda for the extra scrubbing factor. I used a small laundry brush to work the whole concoction into the stain for a few minutes. After that I walked away and let the whole thing sit there for an hour or so, and then laundered as usual.

The difference was amazing and very encouraging. Can't wait to try it on more clothes that have been hiding in my closets and too embarrassed to make an appearance.

tub and shower soap scum buster

I have found some pretty amazing homemade cleaning products over the years, and just when I think there can't possibly be any more, I find something new! But more than finding something *new*, I often find one that works as well and even better than any of the expensive name-brand products.

My friend Julia posted this recipe on Pinterest and raved about it, so I decided to mix up a batch (which is to say I added equal parts of two ingredients to an empty bottle—hardly tricky stuff) and gave it a test-drive.

I didn't have anything in my cleaning bag of tricks that I could use on soap scum in my shower and bath. I really hadn't thought much about cleaning soap scum because it didn't pose a big problem in my shower, since I am conscientious about wiping it down in between uses. But my boys' bathtub/shower was another story! It had a dull layer of soap scum that nothing I tried could penetrate. I decided to give Tub and Shower Magic by Bobbin at Food.com a try.

12 oz white vinegar

24-oz spray bottle

12 oz Dawn dishwashing liquid

Heat the vinegar in the microwave until warm and pour into a spray bottle. Then add the Dawn. Put on the lid and gently shake to mix.

Now it's time to get to work. I let the mixture sit for about an hour while I tended to other chores, and then I decided just to combine my morning shower in the boys' bathroom with the scrubbing portion of this experiment. Sorry. No pictures are available.

Here's the lowdown on this "magical" stuff: It works! It definitely ate through the stubborn soap scum that was pretty much all over the enclosure. Now when I rub my fingers over the surface, it's once again smooooooth and clean feeling, and you can actually see the restored shine.

HOW TO CLEAN YOUR WASHING MACHINE

Clean your washing machine? Sounds kind of unnecessary, doesn't it? Yes, it *sounds* that way, but when you think about all the dirt and grime that cycles through your washer on a day-to-day basis, it actually makes perfect sense. Washers need washing, too!

My washer is actually almost new, so I figured it would be kind of silly to clean it at this point. *Silly* is the word, all right. Silly me. Upon close inspection, I realized the washer could definitely use a cleaning, especially after I started looking under the hood. Oy!

I got to work and filled the washer with hot water. Then I added one quart of chlorine bleach—no detergent—and let the machine agitate for a minute as I set it to the long wash and spin cycle. Then I shut it off and let the bleach and hot water sit for one hour. After one hour, I restarted the machine and let it run through the complete cycle.

Still not done.

Before the machine could take a break, I immediately filled the washer with hot water again and added one quart of distilled white vinegar with the machine set on the longest cycle. Once again, I let it agitate for a minute, then sit for another hour.

While the machine tub is soaking during that one-hour period, dip a scrubber sponge in the vinegar water and detail all the nooks and crannies of your washer, including the knobs, the lid, and the exterior. I used my microfiber cloths to wipe down and then buff the exterior.

If your machine has built-in dispensers, clean those, too. I was fairly shocked at how grimy mine were! The fabric softener and bleach dispensers felt so slimy and just plain icky. (If your dispensers aren't removable, warm one cup of white vinegar in the microwave or in a small saucepan. Pour it into the dispenser and allow it to sit for a few minutes to loosen any buildup.)

Again, after the vinegar hour, let the machine cycle through.

Bleach and vinegar clean away bacteria, soap scum, and mineral deposits from the wash basket and hoses.

This is especially important if you live in a hard-water area. Every washer should be cleaned at least twice per year. If you have hard water, this cleaning process should be done every three months.

This is one of my must-dos when it comes to cleaning. It keeps our trusty washing machines shiny and clean and ready for more use and abuse!

HOW TO CLEAN YOUR DISHWASHER

Someone once asked me about cleaning the inside of the dishwasher. My initial reaction was pretty much the same as it was to washing the washing machine: Why would you wash a washer? Is this really necessary? Sounded mixed up to me. My dishwasher runs practically twenty-four hours a day. How can it possibly be *dirty*?

Well, upon a closer look, it turned out there are *lots* of ways in which it can collect gunk and junk that needs to be cleaned. Tiny bits of food, grease, and soap scum can cling together and get deposited in corners of the dishwasher. Over time, they not only make your dishwasher look and smell bad, they also diminish its efficiency.

All the articles I read on this subject (and there were many) boiled down to basically three or four easy steps:

First: Pull the bottom rack out and examine the drain area and make sure there are no hard chunks that can plug the drain, cause damage to the pump, or scratch dishes. You'd be surprised at what dishwasher repairmen find—bones, crab shells, chips of glass, and even small pieces of gravel. I have no idea where the gravel comes from, but it's there.

Second: Place a dishwasher-safe cup filled with plain white vinegar on the top rack of the dishwasher. Using the hottest water available, run the dishwasher through a cycle—except for the cup of vinegar, the dishwasher needs to be empty. The vinegar helps to wash away the grease and grime, sanitizes, and helps remove the musty odor.

Third: After using the vinegar to sanitize the inside of the dishwasher, sprinkle a cupful of baking soda around the bottom of the tub and run it through the short cycle using the hottest water. The baking soda freshens the musty smell of the dishwasher as well as brightens up the look of the inside of your appliance by removing stains.

Optional: If you have problems with mold and mildew, add one-half to one cup of bleach in the bottom of the dishwasher and run a full cycle. Note: Do not use bleach in your dishwasher if you have a stainless steel interior.

Routine dishwasher cleaning is a good habit to get into. And you have to admit, now that you know how it's done, it's not that hard. My dishwasher is squeaky clean and fresh-smelling, but here are a few important tips to maintain that freshness in between cleanings.

Tips for Maintaining a Clean Dishwasher

- If you have a garbage disposal, run it *before* starting the dishwasher. The dishwasher drains into the same pipe as your sink, so that drain must be clear.
- Run a bit of hot water in your sink before running the dishwasher. You will get cleaner dishes if the water starts hot. You can collect the water you run and use it for watering plants or other purposes.
- Set the thermostat on your water heater to 120°F (50°C). A cooler

water temperature won't do a good job cleaning. Water that is hotter could scald, so be mindful.

- Run full loads to conserve water and energy, but don't pack dishes too tightly. Dishwashers clean dishes by spraying water over them, so the water needs full access on and between the dishes in order to thoroughly clean them.

- If you are inclined to prewash your dishes before you put them in the dishwasher, consider this: Dishwasher detergent *needs* a certain amount of grease and dirt in order to do its job; otherwise, it actually foams up during the cycle, which is not good for your dishwasher.

Now, go forth and clean!

MAKE YOUR OWN GARDENER'S HAND SCRUB

I love a great idea that is both useful for my home and something that makes a great gift as well. This Gardener's Hand Scrub fits the bill perfectly.

Kate at the Gaines Gang (thegainesgang4.blogspot.com) made these as year-end teachers' gifts, but this makes a wonderful gift for anyone who enjoys gardening. Actually, it makes a great gift for anyone who might just get their hands dirty and wants to have them clean and smooth. A lot of women commented that they made the scrub for their mechanic husbands. I use two different sizes of Ball canning jars—eight ounce and twelve ounce—and fill them three-quarters of the way with sugar. I then add Dawn Hand Renewal with Olay Beauty dish soap (the

pink variety) until it reaches just below the bottom of the mouth of the jar.

Stir the sugar and soap together. Continue to add sugar until the mixture has a pastelike consistency. You don't want it to be too runny.

It smells so good, and the light pink color mixed with the white sugar is so pretty.

I add some jute twine as a ribbon, and if I have time, I add a cute label on the jar that says, *To wash the dirt off your hands, use a small amount and rub. The sugar works like an abrasive to remove the dirt, and the soap washes it all away.*

I simply love this hand scrub. It is so great at getting my hands clean, and it makes them feel so soft. If you do a lot of gardening, I highly recommend whipping up a big batch.

TOP THINGS YOU CAN FREEZE TO SAVE TIME AND MONEY

Sometimes I go into what I call "squirrel mode." For example, in the summer I buy large amounts of grapes and freeze them before the season ends. I do not like the grapes that they have in the grocery stores during the winter months, and since frozen is my preferred way of eating these sweet little gems, freezing a bunch for winter is a no-brainer.

Freezing grapes got me thinking about other things that could be

frozen and how much money I could save if I froze things while they were in season, and while a FoodSaver machine is *nice*, researching what I could freeze and how was even more helpful.

Cheese

You can freeze blocks of cheese and they won't crumble if you let them thaw completely before putting them in the fridge. If you prefer to shred your cheese first, add a tablespoon or so of cornstarch or flour to the bag and shake it to prevent clumping when it thaws.

Another great idea is to buy a big piece of Parmigiano Reggiano (the top grade), grate it in the food processor, and put it in a freezer bag. It keeps for months, and all you have to do is open the bag and scoop out a couple of tablespoons when you need it.

Homemade Pancakes, Waffles, and French Toast

Make up a few batches over the weekend for quick defrost-and-go breakfasts during the week. Freeze on a cookie sheet, then toss them in a freezer bag. Reheat in the microwave, toaster, or toaster oven. Way better than the frozen ones you buy in the store.

Fruit

When freezing fruit, it's best to first spread it out on freezer or parchment paper on a cookie sheet, then place it in bags. Individual frozen pieces let you pull out just how much you need.

Try keeping a "smoothie bag" in the freezer. Toss in extra apple wedges, peaches, pears, bananas, melon—any kind of fruit—and use in smoothies.

If you don't like handling mushy bananas, just throw the bananas into the freezer with the skin on. Then when you need them for a recipe (banana bread, anyone?), pull out what you need, microwave for a few seconds, then cut off the top and squeeze the insides into your mixing bowl.

Cooked Rice

Cook a big batch of rice, spread it on a cookie sheet lined with parchment paper, and freeze. When the rice is frozen, just put it in a freezer bag or containers and you have rice in a pinch. Great for brown rice, which takes so long to cook. Use in casseroles, soups, or fried rice.

Pies

Make apple pies in the fall to enjoy throughout the year. Bake and freeze them in freezer bags wrapped in freezer paper. When you have a hankering for pie, take one out of the freezer, remove the wrapping, and place in the oven for two hours at 200 degrees. You can also freeze slices after baking a whole pie. Just don't forget the ice cream on top!

Corn

An easy way to freeze corn on the cob is to put the ears of corn, *without* removing *any* silk or husk, straight into the freezer. When you want to eat it, put it in the microwave just the way you put it in the freezer and cook for five minutes on high for two ears or four minutes for one ear. The silk insulates and protects the corn while it cooks. Tastes like fresh-picked corn!

Tomatoes

Roast Roma tomatoes in the oven at a low temperature (225 degrees) with garlic, fresh herbs, and a drizzle of olive oil for four to five hours. When cooled, transfer to freezer bags. Use them in chili or in your own tomato-based sauces.

Pasta

Whenever you make pasta, go ahead and cook the whole package and freeze any leftovers for later to add to soups and casseroles. Or freeze individual-size portions in a baggie, making sure to squeeze out the air and getting the bag as flat as possible. Reheat by running hot water over the bag for a few minutes.

Flour and Other Grains

Freezing flour and other types of grain that are in the house for at least three days discourages any uninvited "guests" from hatching. You can also store it in the freezer from the get-go, just make sure to double wrap: This prevents condensation and protects it from picking up other freezer smells.

Pesto

Make (or buy) pesto and freeze it in ice-cube trays. Once it's frozen, pop the cubes out and put them in a freezer bag. Nice to have pesto whenever you want it.

Mashed Potatoes

Using an ice cream scoop, put even portions of mashed potatoes onto a parchment-lined cookie sheet. Freeze until hard, then transfer into a freezer bag. Freezing in even portions like this also helps to control how much you are eating. These will keep in the freezer for at least two months.

Cookie Dough

Make a big batch of your favorite cookie dough, scoop onto cookie sheets, and freeze. When the pieces are frozen solid, put them in freezer bags. When you "need" cookies, bake as few or as many as necessary without lots of waste or guilt. Just add one to two minutes to the baking time.

You can also make slice-and-bake cookie dough by shaping the dough into a cylinder and freezing it wrapped in foil.

Soups and Chili

Cool leftover soup completely and transfer to a freezer-friendly container, leaving about one cup of empty space for expansion during freezing. The night before eating, move the container to the fridge to thaw safely, and then reheat and serve.

Broth and Stock

Keep a gallon bag in the freezer and add any leftover veggie pieces, including onion peels, celery stalks, potato peels, etc. When you have enough, make vegetable stock.

Keep another bag for pan drippings or sauces that are left after cooking chicken. This can be used to flavor soups.

Sandwiches

When you pack lunches for school or work, it's a real time-saver to pull a sandwich straight from the freezer. Just throw it into your lunch box/bag in the morning and it's thawed by lunchtime. It also helps keep the meat cold. Peanut butter and jelly or honey, or deli meat and a slice of cheese work well. You can freeze butter or mustard, but not mayo, lettuce, or tomato. Those can be packed separately or added in the morning.

You can also freeze breakfast sandwiches. Cook scrambled eggs and sausage or bacon in bulk, pile them onto biscuits or English muffins, wrap them individually, and then freeze. In the morning grab one out of the freezer, microwave, and enjoy.

Potato Chips, Crackers, and Pretzels

Stock up on chips, crackers, and pretzels when they are on sale and throw them in the freezer. Frozen chips actually taste better. Eat them straight from the freezer. They are crisper and the flavors pop.

Milk

Ever wonder why plastic milk jugs have those circular indents on the sides? They are there to allow milk to expand while freezing. What a revelation!

To use frozen milk, let thaw, and then *shake well* before opening to make sure any solids are remixed.

You can also freeze buttermilk. No more tossing out half a quart because you needed only a cup.

Juice

As with milk, the only concern about freezing juice involves leaving room for expansion. A good rule of thumb is to take out eight ounces for every half gallon of juice. Stock up when it goes on sale or at a discount warehouse.

Baked Goods

When you're in a baking mood, make extras of your favorite baked goods and freeze them for later.

Tip for defrosting baked goods: Place them in your microwave overnight. It keeps them from drying out like they do sitting on the counter.

Buttercream Frosting

Yep. It's true. Freeze leftover frosting (it would be a *crime* to throw any away), and then when you need to frost something (or just need a frosting fix) let it thaw in the fridge, whip it up, and color/decorate as if it were just made.

Tomato Paste

Most recipes using tomato paste call for only one tablespoon out of the whole can. Then you're left with an almost full *open* can. What to do? Put the rest in a little sandwich bag, flatten it out, and put it in the freezer, and when you need a tablespoon, just break off a piece and throw it into whatever you are cooking. Saves money, and the paste lasts forever. Well, maybe not *forever*, but at least a year.

Diced Veggies

Dice onions, chiles, or bell peppers, then freeze flat in gallon freezer bags. As they are freezing, press score lines into the bags so you can break off as much or as little as you wish for recipes.

Homemade and Store-Bought Dough

You can freeze all kinds of homemade dough, shaped in a ball and wrapped in plastic wrap.

You can also freeze canned biscuits, crescent rolls, pizza dough, and so on right in the tube. Stock up when they are on sale.

Eggs

Really? Who would have thought? Crack the eggs in a freezer bag and freeze. Or crack eggs into an ice-cube tray for cakes and cookies. Thaw out in the refrigerator and use as you normally would.

Shredded Chicken

Cook a big batch and shred, or when you buy a rotisserie chicken from the grocery store, shred the leftovers and put them in a bag. Great time-saver when making enchiladas.

Lemon/Lime Juice and Zest

Squeeze lemons and limes into ice-cube trays, then pop them out after they have frozen and store in freezer bags. Now you have "fresh" lemon and lime juice whenever you need it. And you never have to kick yourself for letting another bag of lemons go to waste.

Don't forget to zest the lemons/limes first and keep that in the freezer as well.

Herbs

Freeze fresh herbs in ice-cube trays with a little water or leftover stock to use for soups, stews, and casseroles later in the year. Chop your favorite herbs up into a size that will fit in a cube, then fill each cube to the top with stock or water.

Marinated Meat

Place meat in a freezer bag, pour in marinade, and freeze. When you defrost it, it will be fully marinated and ready to cook.

Homemade Casseroles

When you are cooking casseroles (like lasagna, mac and cheese, or enchiladas), why not make two and freeze one for those times when unexpected company drops by or to use during a busy school/work week?

You can freeze casseroles in two ways:

1. Line the base of the dish with freezer paper, add the ingredients, then freeze it in the dish. When it's frozen solid, remove from the dish (easy to do thanks to the freezer paper), rewrap the food, and put it back in the freezer. This saves room in the freezer and allows you to continue using the dish. When you want the item for a meal, unwrap and place in the original dish to defrost and cook.

2. Bake the casserole, let cool, and then cut into individual servings and freeze. Reheat in microwave.

Fish Sticks

Forget those tasteless sticks in the supermarket freezer section. Buy fresh fish in quantity, cut it crosswise into fish "fingers," dip in egg, dredge in flour and bread crumbs, then freeze laid out on a tray before transferring to freezer bags. So much better than anything you buy in the store.

Hamburger

Don't ever stress about defrosting a pound of hamburger for dinner again. Precook ground hamburger and portion it out for meals. When you need hamburger for shepherd's pie, sloppy joes, tacos, or whatever takes ground beef, pull it out of the freezer, add the seasoning, and microwave. Three minutes, or one and a half minutes if it's going to be baked and doesn't need to be thawed all the way. For Crock-Pot meals, like chili, just throw it in frozen.

Wow . . . who knew you could freeze all of these things? I certainly didn't! Now I just need a decent-size (or second) freezer to put it all in. Definitely on my wish list.

HOW TO UNSHRINK YOUR CLOTHES (YES, THIS IS POSSIBLE!)

I have a sad story, followed by a happy ending.

Some time ago, I went to the Nike Store because Kell needed football cleats. Of course, I ended up browsing in the women's clothing department as well. Although I wasn't looking for anything in particular, I did find myself inexplicably drawn to a pair of royal blue pants (or, as I like to call them, "comfy pants"). I don't usually shop for myself at the Nike

Store, but those pants were calling my name. I just loved the color, and they were made out of the softest T-shirt–like material. So I gave in to the temptation, which was just too great to bear, and purchased the pants.

Here's the sad part of the story: I got to wear them only once before they were ruined by the evil clothes dryer.

Well, it's really not the clothes dryer's fault. I had intended to wash them and then let them air-dry because I feared they might shrink. But the hubster, bless his heart, got to the load of clothes in the washing machine before I did . . . and into the dryer they went.

When I went to take the clothes out of the dryer and saw the blue pants, I wanted to cry. My laundry intuition (something you develop after years and years and years of doing laundry for a family of six) told me they were no longer going to be wearable. Sure enough, they had shrunk in length a good four inches at least.

I dried my bitter tears and decided to chalk it up to experience and put the pair of "floods" into a bag with a bunch of other outgrown T-shirt items that I like to save for future projects. I tried to move on with my life.

I was almost over the whole horrible experience when I got an e-mail from someone asking if I knew how they could unshrink some article of clothing that had shrunk in the dryer. Hmmm . . . sounded familiar. I immediately thought of my blue pants, wadded up in an old pillowcase. Was *unshrinking* even possible? Sounded like some voodoo magic to me. But what the heck, it was worth a try.

So, I researched this magic reversal process and was amazed to discover just how easy it is to unshrink clothing (and that it didn't involve any sort of black magic whatsoever!).

What it does involve is a sink full of lukewarm water, a capful of baby shampoo, and two large beach towels.

Fill a sink with lukewarm water and add a capful of baby shampoo to the water. (Many tutorials I read said to use conditioner, but shampoo made more sense to me, so this is what I used.)

Let the item soak in the baby shampoo water and gently work it through. This will soften the fibers in the clothing.

After five to ten minutes, remove the garment from the shampoo water and gently squeeze it out. Do not rinse it.

Lay the clothing flat on a large towel. Roll the towel up with the clothing inside it. Your goal is to absorb the extra moisture, so your clothing is damp but not wet. Then, get another dry towel and put the piece of clothing out on the dry towel. Gently stretch the clothing item as it lays out to dry. Continue to do this until the clothing item returns to its original size. Allow the item to air-dry on the towel.

Being the impatient person that I am, I set up a fan to make the drying time go faster, and within about an hour or so they were dry. Of course, the fact that we practically live in the Sahara Desert didn't hurt, either.

The anticipation was killing me, so I immediately tried them on. (I guess I had some irrational fear that the stretching I did was an illusion?) When I pulled them on, they were back to the exact same length they were when I bought them, and I was beyond thrilled! My comfy pants were back!

Now I can't help thinking about all the clothes that got thrown away in the past because I did not know this trick. There I go, overthinking again . . .

Do everyone you know a favor and spread the word before more innocent items of clothing meet their premature demise.

DIY SKIN SMOOTHER FOR SILKY-SMOOTH LEGS

Did you know you are supposed to exfoliate your legs? I always assumed that the very act of shaving your legs was exfoliating in itself. Oh, silly me! That kind of low-maintenance personal hygiene has been reserved for the male species.

When I started looking into this whole leg-exfoliation idea, I came across all sorts of homemade exfoliator recipes. Apparently you're sup-

posed to exfoliate each time your shave your legs. Who knew? Obviously not me.

Since I've been doing this, my legs have never felt softer *or* smoother. No kidding.

The recipe is supersimple. The most challenging part for me on this particular day was actually finding time to take a bath, so I made do and used it in the shower instead. This actually worked better for me, since I've never really been a fan of shaving in the bathtub, anyway. All that hair floating around and such. Sorry for the visual!

1¼ cup sugar

½ cup oil (I used olive oil, but you can use any oil—coconut oil, baby oil, canola oil, etc.)

3 tbsp citrus juice (lemon or lime) or 20 drops lemon essential oil

Razor

Mix the sugar, oil, and juice together. I put everything in a mason jar and just shook it all up. If you take the glass jar into the bath or shower with you, please be extra careful since it can be slippery and you are holding glass.

Soak your legs in the tub for 5 minutes. Or if you're taking a shower, wash and condition your hair first, then after your legs have had a chance to soak for a few minutes, apply the mixture to your legs and rub it in. I was surprised at how good this felt. I ended up using it on my feet and arms as well.

The abrasiveness of the sugar rubs off all the dirt and dead skin; the citrus juice works as a mild skin peel, revealing brighter, smoother skin; and, of course, the oil penetrates deep into the skin and provides long-lasting moisture.

After rubbing the mixture in for a few minutes, it's time to shave your legs. Feels pretty good, huh? Well, we're just getting started!

Now, rinse and repeat. Yep, do it again. Rub the mixture all over your legs (and feet). Shave. Rinse again. This time you might want to use a mild soap to get off some of the oil. Or not. Your preference. Note: Make sure the bottom of the shower is oil-free when you are done so the next person who steps in doesn't get a slippery surprise. Since I used body wash after shaving, mine was fine and oil-free.

When you get out of the bath or shower, put lotion on and enjoy your silky-smooooooooth legs. I guarantee you will be so amazed at how soft your skin feels, you won't be able to keep your hands off yourself.

THE ULTIMATE DETOX BATH

When I read that toxins can build up in your body over time and cause myriad uncomfortable symptoms, it struck a chord with me. I decided to give a recommended detoxification bath a try. It couldn't hurt, right? The worst thing that could happen would be a nice, relaxing hot bath and some rare downtime.

Toxins and chemicals are all around us, from our drinking water, to our health and beauty products, to the materials used to build and furnish our homes. They are unavoidable. There are, of course, certain things we can do to cut back on the amount of toxins in our living environments. Eating organically and using natural cleaning, laundry, and health and beauty products are some preventive measures, to name a few.

If you are feeling lethargic or sluggish or you are just experiencing "brain fog," a detox bath is a great way to help your body get rid of toxins and ease some of these symptoms.

Most detox bath recipes I found while researching this topic contained different combinations of the same basic ingredients: Epsom salts, baking soda, and apple cider vinegar. A few others also added essential oils and ginger. But very few contained the "secret ingredient" I'm going to share with you today: clay!

Healing clay has been used for centuries as a form of natural medicine. Taking a therapeutic clay bath is one of the most effective methods in existence to assist in the elimination of toxic substances that have accumulated in the body. It just so happens that my little town is home to Redmond Clay, who markets an all-natural Utah bentonite clay used by the Fremont Indians thousands of years ago.

> 2 cups Epsom salts (or sea salt)—draws out toxins from your body while relieving aches and pains.
>
> 1 cup apple cider vinegar—soothes and softens dry, itchy skin while balancing and neutralizing the body's pH.
>
> ½ cup bentonite clay—stimulates the lymphatic system to deeply cleanse the body's largest breathing organ, the skin. You can find bentonite clay at your local health food store or an online health and wellness source, such as www.redmondclay.com. I've even seen it at Walmart and on Amazon.com.
>
> 5 to 10 drops of your favorite essential oil—lavender, geranium, sandalwood, ylang-ylang, and blue tansy are all known for their detoxifying properties.

Run your bathwater as hot as you like. Add your ingredients and agitate (swish the water around with your hand; if you have a whirlpool tub, that works, too) to let the ingredients dissolve. Soak in the water for 20 to 40 minutes. Drink a full glass of water when you're finished.

Warning: You will be exhausted after your bath, so do this right before bed. I usually feel like a wrung-out dishrag afterward, but in the morning I felt energized, refreshed, and I have a whole new outlook on life.

jillee's gluten-free bread that doesn't suck

One Saturday morning, I declared on Facebook and Instagram that I was going to make a *good* gluten-free bread, even if it killed me! That tells you how desperate I had become to find an answer to this dilemma in our family.

It may not seem like a big thing to those of you who, fortunately, aren't forced to deal with this issue, but you're going to have to trust me on this one, since Kell and I face this every day (along with millions of others), and it is a big deal. When all of the other kids or the rest of the family is eating French toast for breakfast, grilled cheese for lunch, and cheeseburgers for dinner and Kell can't, I am usually not even left with a gluten-free option to pretend with because most of the store-bought gluten-free bread tastes like sandpaper.

I have filled my cart with every gluten-free type of flour on the market that I could find and I have researched recipes online for hours. The quest was in full swing.

Finally, one day after my social media declaration, the stars must have been aligned in my favor, because the recipe that I came up with turned out far better than I ever dreamed.

I won't bore you with a lengthy explanation for why gluten-free baking is so different from traditional baking and what all the different flours are for and what they do and don't do. There are oodles of websites that go into that in detail. An online search is extremely overwhelming, which is why for the *longest* time I stubbornly refused to get into the gluten-free-baking thing. It was just too complicated. But I finally caved for Kell's sake, since relying solely on premixed, prepackaged, or premade gluten-free bread products left us both disappointed.

The first step was to find a gluten-free flour blend to use in my bread. Like I said, there are so many different flour types out there, it's enough to make you want to go screaming into the night.

Rice flour, teff flour, soy flour, corn flour, potato flour, quinoa flour, tapioca flour, almond flour, coconut flour, bean flour . . . See what I mean? How is anyone without a degree in the culinary arts supposed to figure this out? The only answer I have is to find someone whose opinion you trust and see what they have to say about it, which is not an easy task when you don't know anyone.

I am not a gluten-free expert by *any* stretch of the imagination. But I am stating with 100 percent sincerity that this is the best gluten-free bread that I have ever had . . . and I have tried a lot of them. Will I now stop trying? Certainly not.

Like I said, I started out my quest armed with a handful of recipes. One was called Championship Sandwich Bread from www.livingwithout.com. There is no information on why it's a "championship" bread, but it still sounded promising to me as I was grasping at straws. Plus it was pretty straightforward, and on my first foray into this world of gluten-free bread making, I wanted to start with a simple loaf. The artisan stuff could wait.

After reading through all the comments on the original recipe, I picked up some invaluable tips and have incorporated them into my final recipe. It's like I always say: A lot of "my" best ideas on my blog come from my readers.

· gluten-free flour blend ·

This is adapted from a recipe found in Living Without's *Gluten Free & More* (at www.livingwithout.com). I couldn't find potato flour in the store, so I blended up potato flakes in my Blendtec and that worked just fine. The recipe makes 4 cups of flour blend.

1⅓ cups brown rice flour
1⅓ cups tapioca flour/starch
1⅓ cups cornstarch
1 tbsp potato flour

Mix all ingredients together. Now we're ready to make the gluten-free bread.

jillee's gluten-free bread that doesn't suck

Cooking spray

1 packet (2¼ tsp) active dry yeast (not *instant* dry yeast)

2 cups warm water

4 cups Gluten-Free Flour Blend (see page 296)

1 tbsp xanthan gum

1 tbsp gluten-free egg replacer

2 tsp salt

½ cup powdered milk

3 large eggs at room temperature

¼ cup butter at room temperature

2 tsp cider vinegar

⅓ cup honey

A note about replacements: If you are allergic to eggs, you can replace *all* the eggs in the recipe with egg replacer, which I found near the gluten-free flours in my grocery store. Just follow the instructions on the package. You can also make this bread using water or a plain, gluten-free, nondairy milk instead of the powdered milk.

Spray cooking spray into two 8-inch bread pans.

Add the yeast to the warm water and stir until mixed. Set this aside to activate while you mix the other ingredients.

Mix the flour blend, xanthan gum, egg replacer, salt, and powdered milk together in a medium-size bowl and set aside.

Put the eggs (or additional replacer), butter, vinegar, and honey in the bowl of your mixer. With the paddle attachment, mix together for about 30 seconds. The butter will be chunky; that's okay.

Add half the dry ingredients to the egg mixture in the mixer bowl. Mix until just blended, and then add the remaining dry ingredients and mix for another 30 seconds, until blended.

With the mixer on low speed, slowly add the yeast mixture, then turn the mixer to medium-high speed and beat for 4 minutes.

After 4 minutes, your bread dough should resemble thick cake batter.

Spoon the dough into your greased bread pans. Dip your fingers in water and smooth the top of the dough, if desired. Set aside in a warm place to rise for approximately 50 to 60 minutes. While the dough rises, preheat the oven to 375 degrees.

When the dough has risen to about an inch above the top of the pans, place the pans in the oven on the middle rack and bake for 45 to 55 minutes, or until the bread's internal temperature reaches 200 degrees with an instant-read thermometer. (This is very helpful. It's hard to tell when gluten-free bread is done. But if you don't have an instant-read thermometer, you're going to have to use your best guess based on your particular oven.)

Remove the bread from the oven and let cool in the pans for 10 minutes. Then remove the loaves from the pans and place on a rack to cool.

> The anticipation at this point in the process when I made this bread was killing me! So far everything had gone so well, but I was deathly afraid that once I cut into this bread, it was going to be the same bitter disappointment I'd felt so many times before. But I was still hopeful . . .

Allow the bread to cool *completely*. This is important: Don't rush and cut into it while it's still warm or you will flatten it. Then very carefully cut it into slices. This is *also* very important: Let your bread knife do the cutting for you. You provide the sawing action, but let the knife blade do the work. Don't press down, just keep sawing across the top until you get all the way to the bottom of the loaf and hit the cutting board. The bread slices will keep their shape much better this way.

> I immediately slathered a piece with butter and ate it. I almost started crying. But this time they were tears of joy instead of tears of frustration. It tasted like *bread*. Honest-to-goodness bread.
>
> Then I gave a piece to Kell. This was the real test. He
>
> *(continued)*

loved it! After that I tracked down everyone in the house with a mouth and made them try it. (I let my grandpuppy, Milo, off the hook.) Everyone was in 100 percent agreement that if they didn't know it was gluten-free, they would not have been able to tell. V-I-C-T-O-R-Y!

Soon thereafter, we had cheeseburgers for dinner. It was the first time that Kell could remember having a cheeseburger on bread. Talk about a memorable burger!

HYDROGEN PEROXIDE MAGIC

Ever since I started using hydrogen peroxide for just about everything—to get rid of armpit stains, to clean cookie sheets, as a miracle cleaner in my kitchen and bathroom, and to make my own OxiClean—I always keep at least one bottle under each sink in the kitchen, bathrooms, and laundry room. Over the years, I have truly come to realize what a miracle substance hydrogen peroxide really is. It's safe, readily available, cheap, and above all, it works for a lot of stuff.

Hydrogen peroxide should really be called oxygen water, since it is basically the same chemical makeup as water, but with an extra oxygen atom (H_2O_2), and once you have it, you won't be able to go on living without it.

Some other interesting facts about hydrogen peroxide:

- It is found in all living material.
- Your white blood cells naturally produce hydrogen peroxide to fight bacteria and infections.

- Fruit and vegetables naturally produce hydrogen peroxide. This is one of the reasons it is so healthy to eat fresh fruit and vegetables.

- It is found in massive dosages in mother's first milk, called colostrum, and is transferred to the baby to boost the newborn's immune system.

- It is found in rainwater because some of the H_2O in the atmosphere receives an additional oxygen atom from the ozone (O_3), and this H_2O_2 makes plants grow faster.

- Next to apple cider vinegar, hydrogen peroxide ranks up there as one of the best household remedies.

- Besides cleansing wounds, H_2O_2 dissolves earwax, brightens dingy floors, adds natural highlights to your hair, improves plants' root systems . . . the list goes on and on.

There are so many uses for this stuff that I've started replacing the cap on the hydrogen peroxide bottle with a sprayer because it's easier and faster to use that way.

I have compiled a rather impressive list of uses for 3 percent hydrogen peroxide that I hope will have you as thrilled and bewildered as I was.

In no particular order, I present you with:

Jillee's Big List of Uses for H_2O_2

- Wash vegetables and fruits with hydrogen peroxide to remove dirt and pesticides: Add ¼ cup of H_2O_2 to a sink of cold water. After washing produce, rinse thoroughly with cool water.

- In the dishwasher, add two ounces to your regular detergent for a sanitizing boost. Also, beef up your regular dish soap by adding roughly two ounces of 3 percent H_2O_2 to the bottle.
- Use hydrogen peroxide as a mouthwash to freshen breath. It kills the bacteria that cause halitosis. Use a fifty-fifty mixture of hydrogen peroxide and water.
- Use baking soda and hydrogen peroxide to make a paste for brushing teeth. This helps with early stages of gingivitis, as it kills bacteria. Mixed with salt and baking soda, hydrogen peroxide also works as whitening toothpaste.
- Soak your toothbrush in hydrogen peroxide between uses to keep it clean and prevent the transfer of germs. This is particularly helpful when you or someone in your family has a cold or the flu.
- Clean your cutting board and countertop with hydrogen peroxide. Let everything bubble for a few minutes, then scrub and rinse clean.
- Wipe out your refrigerator and dishwasher with it. Because hydrogen peroxide is nontoxic, it's great for cleaning places that store food and dishes.
- Clean your sponges. Soak them for ten minutes in a fifty-fifty mixture of hydrogen peroxide and warm water in a shallow dish. Rinse the sponges thoroughly afterward.
- Remove baked-on crud from pots and pans. Combine hydrogen peroxide with enough baking soda to make a paste, then rub onto the dirty pan and let it sit for a while. Come back later with a scrubby sponge and some warm water, and the baked-on stains will lift right off.

- Whiten bathtub grout. First dry the tub thoroughly, then spray it liberally with hydrogen peroxide. Let it sit—it may bubble slightly—for a little while, then come back and scrub the grout with an old toothbrush. Depending on the level of dinginess, you may have to repeat the process a few times.

- Clean the toilet bowl. Pour half a cup of hydrogen peroxide into the toilet bowl, let it stand for twenty minutes, then scrub clean.

- Remove stains from clothing, curtains, and tablecloths. Hydrogen peroxide can be used as a pretreater for stains—just soak the stain for a little while in 3 percent hydrogen peroxide before tossing the item into the laundry. You can also add a cup of peroxide to a regular load of whites to boost brightness. It's a green alternative to bleach, and works just as well.

- Brighten dingy floors. Combine half a cup of hydrogen peroxide with one gallon of hot water, then go to town on your flooring. Because it's so mild, it's safe for any floor type, and there's no need to rinse.

- Clean kids' toys and play areas. Hydrogen peroxide is a safe cleaner to use around kids, or anyone with respiratory problems, because it's not a lung irritant. Spray toys, toy boxes, doorknobs, and anything else your kids touch on a regular basis.

- Help out your plants. To ward off fungus, add a little hydrogen peroxide to your spray bottle the next time you're spritzing plants.

- Add natural highlights to your hair. Dilute the hydrogen peroxide so the solution is 50 percent peroxide and 50 percent water. Spray the solution on wet hair to create subtle, natural highlights.

- According to alternative-therapy practitioners, adding half a bottle of hydrogen peroxide to a warm bath can help detoxify the body. Some are skeptical of this claim, but a bath is always a nice way to relax, and the addition of hydrogen peroxide will leave you—and the tub—squeaky clean!

- Spray a solution of one-half cup water and one tablespoon of hydrogen peroxide on leftover salad, drain, cover, and refrigerate. This will prevent wilting and better preserve your salad.

- Sanitize your kids' lunch boxes/bags.

- Dab hydrogen peroxide on pimples or acne to help clear skin.

- Hydrogen peroxide helps to sprout seeds for new plantings. Use a 3 percent hydrogen peroxide solution once a day and spritz the seeds every time you remoisten. You can also use a mixture of 1 part hydrogen peroxide to 32 parts water to improve your plants' root system.

- Remove yellowing from lace curtains or tablecloths. Fill a sink with cold water and two cups of 3 percent hydrogen peroxide. Soak for at least an hour, rinse in cold water, and air-dry.

- Use it to remove earwax. Use a solution of 3 percent hydrogen peroxide with olive or almond oil. Add a couple drops of oil first, then H_2O_2. After a few minutes, tilt head to remove solution and wax.

- Helps with foot fungus. Spray a fifty-fifty mixture of hydrogen peroxide and water on your feet (especially the toes) every night and let dry. Or try soaking your feet in a peroxide solution to help soften calluses and corns and disinfect minor cuts.

- Spray down the shower with hydrogen peroxide to kill bacteria and viruses.

- Use one pint of 3 percent hydrogen peroxide to a gallon of water to clean humidifiers and steamers.

- Wash shower curtain liners with hydrogen peroxide to remove mildew and soap scum. Place liner in washing machine with a bath towel and your regular detergent. Add one cup 3 percent hydrogen peroxide to the rinse cycle.

- Use on towels that have become musty smelling: one-half cup hydrogen peroxide and one-half cup vinegar. Let stand for fifteen minutes, then wash as normal, and that musty smell is gone.

- Deskunking solution. Combine 1 quart 3 percent H_2O_2, ¼ cup baking soda, 1 teaspoon Dawn dish detergent, and 2 quarts warm water.

ORIGINAL BLUE DAWN . . . IT'S NOT JUST FOR DISHES ANYMORE

Here is my list of the "best of the best" ingenious uses for original blue Dawn, gleaned from dozens of websites and readers' comments.

Bubbles

According to www.bubbles.org, Dawn dishwashing liquid makes great homemade bubbles. Here is the giant bubble recipe used in bubble makers at many children's museums: ½ cup Dawn; ½ gallon warm water; 1 tablespoon glycerin (available at any drugstore) or light corn syrup. Stir gently. Skim the foam off the top of the solution (too much foam breaks down the bubbles). Dip the bubble wand and get ready for some good, clean fun.

Greasy Hair Problems

Kids get into the darnedest things! Like Vaseline and baby oil rubbed into their hair. Dawn is mild enough to use on their hair and strong enough to remove the most stubborn grease.

Hair Product Buildup

Once a month use original Dawn as you would shampoo. It will remove excess oil from your hair and scalp and strip away any buildup of styling products without any damage. Perform this once a month and you won't have to buy expensive salon products that do the same thing.

At-Home Manicure Secret

Soak fingers in full-strength blue Dawn. It makes the cuticles soft and easy to work with. And it removes the natural oil from the fingernails, which allows the polish to adhere very well.

Repel Houseplant Insects

A safe, effective way to repel insects from your houseplants, such as aphids, spider mites, and mealy bugs. Put a drop of Dawn dishwashing liquid in a spray bottle, fill the rest of the bottle with water, shake well, and mist your household plants with the soapy water.

Clean Your Windows

Try this recipe from Merry Maids: Mix three drops of Dawn in one gallon of water and fill a spray bottle with the solution. Spritz and wipe as you would with any window cleaner.

Pests on Pets

Use it to bathe the dogs. It kills fleas on contact and is much cheaper than expensive dog shampoos.

Clean Automotive Tools

After you have finished your automotive repair project, soak your dirty tools in Dawn before you put them away to remove all the oil and grime. Dawn also helps to prevent rust from forming on the tools.

Ice Pack

Partially fill a strong ziplock sandwich bag with Dawn dishwashing liquid, close, and freeze. The liquid soap stays cold much longer and can be refrozen many times. It will conform to the place you need an ice pack, like your knee, ankle, or forehead.

Tub and Shower Cleaner

Take a microwave-proof spray bottle and fill it halfway with white vinegar. Heat in the microwave for about thirty seconds. Fill the rest of the bottle with blue Dawn. Put the lid on and shake to mix well. Spray on your tub and shower walls. Allow to sit for a few minutes, then rinse away. This solution will totally melt all the gunk, slime, sludge, and other stuff that builds up, including a bathtub ring.

Ant Repellant

Spray countertops, cupboards, and any other area where you see ants with a solution of half Dawn and half water and wipe dry. The slight residue of Dawn that remains will not be a problem at all for kids or pets, but ants hate it. Should you see a trail of ants, go ahead and hit them directly with the Dawn spray.

Stripping Cloth Diapers

Put diapers in the washer and add a squirt or two of original Dawn dish soap and run through a hot wash cycle. Rinse until there are no more bubbles and the water runs clear. Dawn is a degreasing agent and helps stripping by removing oily residue.

Unclogging Toilets

A cup of Dawn detergent poured into a clogged toilet and allowed to sit for fifteen minutes, followed with a bucket of hot water poured from waist height in a steady stream right into the center of the bowl to avoid splashing, will clear out the toilet.

Poison Ivy

Poison ivy spreads through the oil within the blisters. Washing the affected area with Dawn, especially on children who keep scratching the blisters open, helps dry up the fluid and keeps the rash from spreading.

Driveway Cleaner

If you have gasoline or motor oil stains on your driveway, you can use kitty litter to soak up the excess oil and then use a scrub broom and a solution of biodegradable Dawn dishwashing detergent and warm water to safely and effectively remove the rest from the pavement.

Paint or Grease Remover for Hands

Dawn combined with corn oil makes for the perfect paint or grease remover. Simply combine a little bit of both in your hands, then rub it over affected areas. The corn oil and the dishwashing liquid both help to dissolve the grease and paint while also leaving skin soft, unlike harsher paint removers.

Cleaning the Kiddie Pool

Plastic wading pools can get gunky very fast. Dump the water, then scrub the pool with Dawn and a sponge. More potent cleaners like bleach will weaken and dry out the plastic in the sun.

Multipurpose Cleaner

Merry Maids recommends using a drop of Dawn in a gallon of water to clean ceramic tile and no-wax/linoleum floors. You can also use the spray on:

Bathroom and kitchen counters and sinks

Woodwork (Be careful to dry as you go, since wood doesn't like prolonged contact with water.)

Tubs and toilet seats

Laundry Pretreatment for Oily Stains

For oil-based stains such as lipstick, grease, butter, motor oil, cooking oil, and some inks, simply apply some Dawn dishwashing liquid directly to the stain, scrub with a small brush or toothbrush until the oil is removed, and then launder as usual.

Nontoxic Lubricant

Use Dawn directly on sliding glass doors, doorknobs, hinges, etc. It lasts much longer than any aerosol spray that I have tried. And it's nontoxic. It does a great job of cleaning the parts that it's lubricating as well.

Sidewalk Deicer

For icy steps and sidewalks in freezing temperatures, mix 1 teaspoon of Dawn dishwashing liquid, 1 tablespoon of rubbing alcohol, and ½ gallon of hot/warm water and pour over walkways. They won't refreeze. No more salt eating at the concrete in your sidewalks or driveway.

Pool Cleaner

Squirt Dawn down the middle of the pool, and all of the dirt and oils from suntan lotions and sunblocks will move to the edges of the pool for easy cleanup. And it makes the pool sparkle.

Eyeglass Defogger

Simply rub a small drop of Dawn on eyeglass lenses and wipe clean. It will leave a very thin film that will prevent them from fogging up.

Shower Floors

Cover greasy footprints on shower floors with a coating of Dawn; let sit overnight. Scrub away the gunk in the morning with a stiff brush.

Aphid Control on Fruit Trees

Mix 2 tablespoons Dawn to 1 gallon of water and put in your sprayer. Try to get spray on both sides of the leaves, branches, and tree trunks. Let sit for about 15 minutes, and then rinse the trees thoroughly.

LESSONS I WANT MY KIDS TO LEARN
(AND YOUR KIDS, TOO)

Obviously, wanting to teach our children is not a new concept. But understand that after everything I have personally been through, one good thing that has never changed is the absolute love and devotion I have for my children. For me, this is really not even just one good thing, but the one greatest thing of all: the ability to teach our children. It was and remains my fierce love and desire to protect them that made me triumph and overcome my addiction. Of course, I cannot forget Dave, who did double duty as a loving parent while I was gone. I count my blessings daily because my children have come through this odyssey fairly unscathed. I know it's not possible to shield them from the life lessons that they must learn on their own, but I would like to share with them (and with you) some of the things that I think will help them live their own good lives. It goes without saying that my children will make their own mistakes, and I will be here as long as I can to catch them when they fall, as my parents were for me. Funny thing is, these lessons can still be applied to us adults. It's never too late to learn.

Don't get into debt. Money problems ruin many relationships.

Start saving early! Not only is it easier to make it a habit, but the compound interest will make your retirement much more comfortable.

Don't be a bully. Better than that, go the extra mile to befriend the "outsider."

Explore your creative side. You were given unique and wonderful talents. Don't let them go to waste.

Choose your profession carefully. Try to find your passion early so you never have to "work" a day in your life.

Take time to smell the roses. Life goes by too fast (especially once you get married and start a family).

Always say "Thank you."

Respect your elders.

Depression and anxiety are not something to be ashamed of. If you struggle with it, get help.

Laugh! The ability to laugh easily and frequently improves your relationships and your health.

If addiction runs in your family, don't tempt fate. You don't need alcohol or drugs to have a good time.

The best thing you can do for your children is to love and respect your spouse.

Kell, Britta, Neil, me, Dave, Sten, Erik, and Kaitlyn

Give back to your community.

Remember compliments you receive and forget the insults. As my kids are fond of saying, "Haters gonna hate."

Always remember that no one owes you a living. You are responsible for doing what it takes to get the things you want and need.

Love and sex are not like in the movies. There is no such thing as "happily ever after" unless you work at it constantly.

Choose a spouse who is your best friend. I did, and despite a few detours along the way, it's worked out pretty well.

Always look for opportunities to do service. It can be as simple as holding the door open for someone, but it's amazing the good feelings that come from it, both for them and for you.

Don't judge. Not ever.

Love unconditionally. And just in case you're wondering what that means . . . it means absolutely and without conditions or limitations. Period.

For me and my children, having a relationship with God is important. For you and yours, belief systems are still essential.

And the most important thing I want my kids to remember is always call home. After all, that's where the heart is.

acknowledgments

I want to express my heartfelt gratitude to some of the people in my life who have been with me along this journey and have all played a part in helping me through.

First of all, my love and gratitude to my husband, Dave, for refusing to give up on that girl he met in Bismarck; and to my children, for being my reason for living during the darkest days and my greatest joy each day. And thanks for marrying Kaitlyn and Neil—a mother-in-law couldn't ask for more.

Thank you to my parents, Carole and Richard Warner, whose unconditional love has been a guiding star throughout my life; and to my sisters, Rebecca, JoAnn, and Dori, who are my best friends in the world. Also, my appreciation to my brothers, Cole and Kevin, my defenders and shining examples.

My appreciation to my family team: my nephew, Scott Warner, for believing that One Good Thing by Jillee could be so much more. And to Britta, Kaitlyn, and Erik for helping to make that happen.

Thanks to all my other nieces and nephews who make me laugh and bring me endless joy.

My everlasting gratitude to the Ark of Little Cottonwood—especially Gloria and Laura Boberg—and all the other "guests" who, for seventy-eight days, were my surrogate family and helped me to find myself again.

Thank you to all the people in the "rooms" of Alcoholics Anonymous for being my lighthouse when I was caught in a raging storm.

My gratitude to my literary agent, Steve Troha at Folio Literary Management, and his assistant, Nikki Thean, for believing in the value of One Good Thing by Jillee as a story that needed to be told.

Thanks to Putnam and my editor, Kerri Kolen, who believed that my humble story should be a book.

At BlogHer, my appreciation to Lisa Stone, Elisa Camahort, Jory Des Jardins, Jenny Lauck, and Susan Getgood, for supporting the growth and success of my blog.

To my church congregation, the Heber City 9th Ward of the Church of Jesus Christ of Latter-day Saints, thank you for being my family's guardian angels when I was going through rehab and never letting me forget I was loved and valued for who I was.

My appreciation to literary agent Marcy Posner at Folio, who brought me to Stephanie Gertler. My very special thanks to Stephanie, whose assistance with the writing of this book was invaluable and inspirational. In addition to writing (and correcting my punctuation), she lent a listening ear and a shoulder to cry on—and we laughed so much. Most important, we became new and lifelong friends.

Finally, thanks to my blog readers. Your inspiration and encouragement are the reasons I continue to look for that one good thing.